BROWN ALE

The Classic Beer Style Series is devoted to offering in-depth information on world-class styles by exploring their history, flavor profiles, brewing methods, recipes, and ingredients.

BROWN ALE

History, Brewing Techniques, Recipes

Ray Daniels and Jim Parker

Classic Beer Style
Series no. 14

Brewers Publications
A Division of the Brewers Association
Boulder, Colorado

Brewers Publications, Division of the Brewers Association
PO Box 1679, Boulder, CO 80306-1679
(303) 447-0816; Fax (303) 447-2825
BrewersAssociation.org

Printed in the United States of America
10   9   8   7   6   5   4   3

ISBN-13: 978-0-937381-60-1
ISBN-10: 0-937381-60-8

Please direct all inquiries to the above address.

Library of Congress Cataloging-in-Publication Data
Daniels, Ray.
    Brown ale : history, brewing techniques, recipes / Ray Daniels and Jim Parker
        p.   cm. — (Classic beer style series ; 14)
    Includes bibliographical references and index.
    ISBN 0-937381-60-8 (alk. paper)
    1. Ale. I. Parker, Jim, 1960– II. Title. III. Series.
    TP578 .D36   1998
    641.2´3—ddc21   98-30008
                                                              CIP
                                                              r98

To my parents, Jon and Phyllis Daniels.
Little did they know they were raising a brewer.

With love to my son, Joel Parker.

Contents

Contents

Acknowledgments

We have worked together in various ways over the past few years, but this book is our first collaborative effort at writing a major document. Past meetings—from the Red Fish in Boulder to the red light* bars in Tokyo—have generally ended up being more profitable for the bars and brewers than for our own collaborations. (*In Japan, red lanterns denote drinking establishments, not flesh merchants!). Even some of our serious efforts to get together on this project got way-laid by other beery priorities. In the end, this book evolved from both specific research and our own knowledge and experience with the style. Many people helped along the way.

From Ray: I thank my wife Laura, my daughter Megan, and my son, Jim, for giving me up on those beautiful days during the final crunch.

From Jim: Special thanks to my son, Joel, for putting up with me when I locked myself in my room to write.

Thanks to the Newcastle Brown Ale Web site (http://www.broon.co.ale.uk) for the last three recipes in chapter 6.

Acknowledgments

Last but not least, the following breweries were kind enough to share their recipes for our analysis of commercial brown ales: Bray's Brewpub in Naples, Maine; Free State Brewing Company in Lawrence, Kansas; Brewmaster's in Cincinnati, Ohio; Magnolia Pub and Brewery in San Francisco, California; Jaxon's Restaurant and Brewing Company in El Paso, Texas; Saint Arnold Brewing Company in Houston, Texas; Pyramid Breweries Inc. in Seattle, Washington; Brooklyn Brewing Company in Brooklyn, New York; Great Lakes Brewing Company in Cleveland, Ohio; Goose Island Brewing Company in Chicago, Illinois; Pete's Brewing Company in Palo Alto, California; Midnight Sun Brewing Company in Anchorage, Alaska. Thanks to each of these organizations and their brewers for taking time out to help us.

Introduction

Brown ales cover a wide spectrum of beer flavors. In the broadest sense, they include not only those beers still made in England and the interpretations fermented in North America, but you can also count Scottish ales, several different types of brown ale found in Belgium, and even the brownish *alts* from Germany.

Still, everyone knows that "brown ale" refers first to the English style. Thus, the assignment to write this book was a bit like an entertainment reporter being assigned to the Rodney Dangerfield beat. It's old, everybody knows something about it, but it's also quirky and hard to get a handle on—a bit like grabbing at smoke. (In fact, a lot like it, as you will soon see.)

In truth, however, the beer we now identify as English brown ale does have a distinctive story all its own. It's the tale of a beer born of necessity that helped spawn the development of one of the world's other classic beer styles, porter. It's the story of how the popularity of porter nearly killed brown ale and how porter's own decline led to a revival of brown ale. And it's the story of how a beer that is not held in much regard in its home country has found new life, or lives, in the United States, where homebrewers and craftbrewers have put their own unique stamp on this classic style.

For those already proficient in brewing ale, the production of brown ales can be comfortable and familiar. Standard equipment and ingredients can be readily employed to make a tasty brown ale. But brown ale is not without its mysteries and surprises. Our review of the historical record and the modern-day producers will introduce aspects of brewing that are unknown to most brewers today.

As a result of the long history and widespread interpretation of the style, brown ale allows a brewer endless opportunities for exploration. Start with myriad malts; throw in hops from England, America, and even Germany; supplement with the richly hued sugars of molasses; and spice it all with the likes of cardamom and coriander from the pre-hop days of brewing. Best of all, extract homebrewers can accomplish just as many successful batches as all-grain professionals.

So, while brown ale's past may be somewhat elusive and its present somewhat complex, its future is bright. In today's beer world, few other beer styles hold more potential for exploration and enjoyment. As a result, it is destined to survive and thrive with brewers and lovers of brown ale.

CHAPTER 1

The History of Brown Ale

While exploring the history of brown ale, we wound up visiting nearly every other style of British ale. From mild and pale to porter and stout, and even old ale, they all have some bearing on the development of brown ale. As we discovered the origins of brown ale, we learned a lot about some of these other styles as well. Let us start at the beginning.

Searching for the Earliest Browns

Most brewers writing about the history of beer build a wall near the beginning of the eighteenth century. The "invention" of pale malt is often placed at about this time (circa 1680 to 1700) and tied to the introduction of coke as a smokeless, controllable fuel source. Prior to that, many believe, *all* beers were smoky and brown because malts were dried over a wood fire.

Because of this belief, any examination of brown ale must naturally begin with the earliest recorded days of brewing in Britain. The earliest text dedicated to brewing is dated 1691, so efforts to understand this period present some distinct challenges. Rather than relying on the words of brewers, as we can with most beer history from 1700 on, we must delve into the more general work of historians and the few available works that have dealt with brewing as a part of medieval and pre-industrial life in Britain.

Despite these challenges, some useful insights are available. As a result, you not only can reach a better understanding of the early days of brown ale, but also can see rather clearly that all ales *were not* brown and smoky.

Diversity from the Beginning

The earliest reference to beer in the British Isles comes more than a millennium before the magic date of 1700. Arnold quotes the terms of a lease from 688 whereby payments were to include "12 casks of strong ale, 30 casks of small ale."[1] This passage not only confirms brewing activity at this early date but also provides evidence that different types or styles of ale were made much earlier than the eighteenth century. From this alone, we have reason to doubt whether all beers brewed before 1700 could have been identical in character.

A monk wets his whistle with a cask-conditioned ale.

The key to discovering the origins of brown ale is malt. The color and flavor of malt dictates the character of the finished beer more than any other ingredient or process. In the seminal work of modern malting, Stopes, writing in 1885, praises monastic brewing before 1300, noting that the reverend fathers "loved their nut-brown ale."[2] In this unreferenced observation, Stopes was almost certainly speculating based on a cursory review of history and his own beliefs. Still, it puts a color on ale at an early date. No evidence is found that contradicts this characterization until some time later.

In discussing late-medieval brewing, Corran, in his *History of Brewing*, mentions several points that indicate lighter-colored ales existed. First, he mentions that unmalted grain was used "to a considerable extent, more than would be reckoned judicious today."[3] Ales brewed with a significant amount of unmalted grain would be paler than those brewed with malt alone, no matter the color of the malt.

The use of grains other than barley was also common in the medieval times. Corran tells us that "monks at St. Paul's Cathedral made beer using equal quantities of barley and wheat plus some oats."[4] If malted, the wheat and oats might have been kiln-dried and thus just as smoky and dark as the barley malt. Still, many color compounds come from the barley husk, so in the absence of charring the wheat and oats on the kiln, such high proportions of wheat would tend to produce a lighter-colored product.

At times, wheat was almost certainly used as the only grain in making beer. In 1302, wheat was considerably cheaper than barley and "the price of beer made from wheat malt was only 1-1/2d per gallon."[5] Furthermore, it appears this use of wheat and oats was widespread. Judith Bennett, in one of the most carefully researched reviews of brewing during this period, provides the following:

> Barley, which would become the favored brewing grain of the sixteenth century, was

by no means preferred in the early fourteenth
century; many brewers used more oats than
barley, and wheat and dredge (a combination
of oats and barley) were also sometimes
malted. The use of oats in brewing has been
particularly associated with west country
brewers, but in the thirteenth and early fourteenth centuries, even brewers in London
preferred oats above all other grains.[6]

Finally, Corran comments on the medieval brewing
process: "For light-colored beer, the wort was moved at
once after boiling, but for brown beer it was boiled for
several hours."[7] This provides the most direct statement
yet that paler beers were produced during this period. Of
course, it also reiterates that at least some of the products
were brown. What is harder to divine is the *nature* of these
early brown ales.

Before the ravages of the Black Plague (1348 to
1349), brewing was a domestic occupation practiced primarily, and perhaps exclusively, by women.[8] The word *ale*
identified malt beverages brewed without hops. Instead,
various herbs and spices were used to provide bitterness
and flavor to contrast the sweetness of malt. Although
Corran cites their strengths at 4 to 6% alcohol by volume

(ABV),[9] some, perhaps most, would have been stronger. Bennett describes these drinks: "Made with only malt, water and yeast, English ale was sweeter and less stable than beers brewed on the continent, where hops were added to the process."[10] (Bennett neglects to mention the use of spices, common additives at the time.)

The poor stability of ales in general is well documented. Bennett notes that it was "fast to sour, lasting for only a few days."[11] In the footnotes, she cites a source as saying that consumption would begin as quickly as 12 hours after brewing. This quick use appears to have been a major factor in the character of domestic ale production. Rapid spoilage meant that ale could not be kept in inventory or transported any significant distance for sale. Thus, brews of any size would outstrip the needs of the household, thereby prompting the brewster to quickly sell ale to neighbors and townspeople. The scope of commercialization of ale remained limited by its short life and poor transportability.

Bennett also points out that the efforts of early brewsters were sporadic. Some brewed only once or twice a year, while others continued for a few months and then ceased altogether. Few brewed regularly for many years on end. Further, each followed his or her own recipe and procedures in brewing, thereby introducing myriad variations.

All of this, combined with the domestic nature of the art, leads to another important conclusion. That is, the nature of medieval ale probably varied widely, not only from town to town, but also from week to week within a town and even within the same neighborhood.

A good modern example of this diversity in a common food product is Thanksgiving turkey stuffing. Some elements (both ingredients and processes) are common among many makers. Yet many other elements—ingredients, preferences, and skills—differ. Thus, among the millions of stuffings made each year, an incredibly wide variety of flavors and appearances can be found. If we were to poll 20 people on the color of stuffing, we would probably get a whole rainbow of answers. Similarly, our efforts to pin down the color of medieval ale ends with only the broadest generalizations.

Malt: Be It Ever So Brown and Smoky?

In the time between the end of the Black Death in 1349 and the creation of porter in 1720, the nature of brewing in Britain changed considerably. The most important issues in efforts to understand this period relate to the character and use of the key ingredient, malt.

Throughout this time there are indications that many brewers—even household-based ale-wives—made their own malt. And malt lies at the heart of the brown ale issue. If the malt was brown, then the ales and beers made from it would likely be the same.

In surviving texts and recipes before 1700, the ingredient "malt" is listed with no further distinction or description. It is given as neither "pale" nor "brown," just as malt. For instance, a recipe dating to the early 1500s calls for "10 quarters of malt, 2 quarters of wheat and 2 of oats."[12]

Prior to the development of coal and coke as fuels, pre-industrial malts were dried in some other way. One option was natural drying under the sun. This technique certainly would have produced a very pale malt. Still, its utility would have been limited to the warmer months of the year, and even then it would have depended on the vagaries of English weather.

Kiln drying was probably employed in most cases. Various sources discuss the use of wood, straw, and fern as fuel for the kiln. Each of these brought different features to the kilning and to the finished malt itself.

As for the smokiness that might have been imparted to the malts—no matter their color—there is frequent evidence that it was unwanted, if not entirely avoided. Andrew Boorde described in 1542 the desirable properties of ale: "It must be freshe and cleare, it must not be ropy nor smoky."[13]

Corran notes that during the sixteenth century, "Wood or straw was used for drying, the latter being preferred."[14] Further, some malt from this time must have been fairly pale. In 1577, William Harrison's *Description of England* covered malt and malting: "The best malt is tried by the hardness and color for if it look fresh with a yellow hue, and will write like a piece of chalk after you have bitten a kernel asunder—you may assure yourself it is dried down."[15] As for the making of this malt, Harrison said, "The straw-dried is the most excellent. For the wood-dried malt, when it is brewed, beside that the drink is higher [darker] of color, it doth hurt and annoy the head of him that is not used thereto, because of the smoke."[16] And finally, he describes ale as being "clear and well colored . . . yellow as the gold noble. . . ."[17]

From these descriptions, it seems apparent that a paler sort of malt was being made before coke came along. Apparently the selection of straw versus wood has some effect in that regard. Stopes quotes long passages from the 1750 edition of the *London and Country Brewer* that supports this conclusion, including: "Next to the Coak-dried Malt, the Straw-dried is the sweetest and best tasted: This, I must own, is sometimes well malted, where the Barley, Wheat, Straw, Conveniences, and the Maker's Skill are good."[18]

The kiln's design also influences malt character. Beginning in the early 1600s, there are references to kilns that prevent contact of smoke and malt. The 1615 treatise by Gervase Markham describes a "French kiln" that burns "any kind of fuel whatsoever, and neither shall the smoke offend or breed ill taste in the malt, nor yet discolor it, as many times it doth in open kilns."[19] This is followed by the "West Country kiln made at the end of a kitchen range or chimney, which dries the malt by hot air, with no smoke."[20]

Finally, Corran reviews brewing-related patents given out during the seventeenth century:

> The first patent in any subject connected with brewing appeared in 1634. And altogether fourteen appeared before the end of the century. The interesting point is that thirteen out of the fourteen deal with fuel and heating problems. We may draw the following conclusions from them:
>
> 1. That smoke was a great nuisance in the drying of malt.
> 2. The ale and beer brewed from smoked malt was "unsavoury and unwholesome," but presumably must have been accepted to some extent.

3. The straw, wood, peat and turf were being supplanted by coal, both in the drying of malt and hops and in the boiling of coppers.[21]

These examples indicate that smoky-flavored, brown-colored ales must have existed in pre-industrial Britain. But they also indicate that many brewers and consumers disliked smoke—and to a lesser degree, brown color—and sought to remove these properties from their malts and beers. No doubt, some succeeded. As a result, ales both pale and lacking in smoke must have been available to some significant extent long before 1700.

With Hops Comes Beer

Between the end of the Black Plague and the development of porter, many changes in beer and brewing occurred. None were more significant than the use of hops. The use of hops—and the British resistance to them—can be credited with several of the anomalies found in our culture today. More important, the introduction of hops created beer—as distinct from unhopped ale. With this new beverage came many other changes in the production and consumption of fermented grain beverages in Britain.

According to Bennett, hops may have been introduced to Britain as early as the late thirteenth century.[22]

But that early exposure didn't take. It was not until almost 100 years later that beer established a firm beachhead in the towns of southeast England. It would take nearly 400 years for beer to fully prevail and for the linguistic distinction of ale as an unhopped beverage to disappear.

Beer came from the European continent, and in those early centuries, most was made by Dutch or Flemish emigrants. One group of new arrivals to Britain settled in East Kent County in 1524.[23] There, they planted hops, founding what has become England's most famous hop-growing region.

Gathering the Hoppe.

"Cutte them" (the hop stalkes) "a sunder wyth a sharpe hooke, and wyth a forked staffe take them from the Poales."

The use of hops brought many advantages to brewers. First and foremost, hops helped prevent spoilage. In so doing, they brought new options and alternatives to brewers. Reginald Scot extolled the virtues of hops, circa 1576: "If your ale may endure a fortnight, your beer through the benefit of the hop, shall continue a month, and what grace it yieldeth to the taste, all men may judge that have sense in their mouths."

Now that beer brewers could rely on hops rather than alcohol as a preservative, they made products that were lower in original gravity (OG) and lower in alcohol compared to the ales of the time. Says Bennett, "Adding hops to the brewing process also gave beer brewers more drink for their grain. Ale brewers generally drew about 7-1/2 gallons from a bushel of malt, brewing their drink strong in order to improve longevity. Yet, because seething the wort in hops assisted both fermentation and preservation, beer brewers were able to achieve the same effect with less grain."[24] Bennett quotes Scot as making "8 or 9 gallons of indifferent ale out of one bushel of malt," but "18 or 20 gallons of very good beer."[25]

Beers took somewhat longer to mature than ales, but once ready, they remained in good condition much longer. Bennett provides a description from *Five Hundred Points of Good Husbandry*, by Thomas Tusser, circa 1580:

"Too new is no profit, too stale is as bad. Ideally, both ale and beer were sold when solidly 'stale'—neither new and unmatured nor old and soured." This ideal moment varied with strength; if a brewer produced an exceptionally strong batch of either ale or beer, it took longer to mature, but once properly stale, it lasted longer in that state. Beer was usually not ready for sale until about a week after brewing, but it improved with age and could be kept for as long as a year.[26]

Clearly, beer brewers held an advantage in the basic economics of their trade. Not only could they make twice as much beer from the same amount of malt compared to an ale brewer, but their product lasted much longer, thereby providing more opportunities for sales. As one result of this disparity, regulations issued in 1531 set a barrel of beer equal to 36 gallons, while a barrel of ale was said to be 32 gallons.[27] This disparity survives today in that Britain's brewers still use 36-gallon barrels, while U.S. brewers use a measure close to that once set for ale, 31-gallon barrels.

For quite some time, beer was priced lower than ale, and this no doubt helped the conversion of the drinking public from ale to beer. But many other changes resulted from the coming of beer. For example, brewing shifted away from the domestic and often occasional trade of women to being the task primarily of men, who may have been lured into full-time brewing by the greater opportunity for profit offered by a stable, higher-margin product. With this change came others, including the separation of selling and brewing among different parties, the gradual disappearance of occasional home-based commercial brewing, and the evolution of common victualers, "who baked bread, brewed drink and managed alehouses."[28]

These early beers probably showed the same variations in color and smokiness as their ale-like brethren. Many of the citations given previously in the chapter related to beer as well as ale. Thus, as early as 1400, there may have been an English beverage that resembled what is today thought of as brown ale. More remarkably, products resembling today's pale ales may have been produced at about the same time.

The Spice of Life

Accepting for the moment that at least some pre-industrial ales were brown—and more or less smoky—we want to review a final issue. The unhopped ales of the time were not made with malt, water, and yeast alone. To counter the sweetness of the malt, ale brewers added herbs and spices of various kinds. In attempting to characterize this practice, we again meet the concept of variety, as introduced in our turkey stuffing example.

No doubt, the herbs that were used in making ale varied widely based on locale, season, and personal taste. One view of hops is that they were simply another spice that brewers found convenient to use. The novelty of hops comes from the fact that they emerged as a defining ingredient of beer, ultimately winning out over all other additives. Still, the triumph of hops was long in the making. Even after every brew included hops, some brewers still found reasons to include special spices.

Bennett lists spices that appear to date from fifteenth-century brews, including "ginger, gillyflower, mountain thyme, and curcuma." The use of ginger was probably quite common and popular, as evidenced by the modern availability of "ginger ale." Gillyflower, or clove gillyflower, may have referred at the time to cloves, although today it is recognized as a species altogether different from the clove. Some types of this pink flower are poisonous.[29] Curcuma is turmeric, according to the *Oxford English Dictionary*.[30]

The list of herbs used seems endless. In *A Sip through Time,* Cindy Renfrow lists not only the herbs but also complete recipes for the brewing of pre-industrial beers.[31] She offers herb-spiked recipes dating to 1577. One uses hops but also includes bay and laurel berries and orris root and notes that long pepper may be used instead of these.[32] A second calls for cinnamon, cloves, nutmeg, long pepper, licorice, ginger root, grains of paradise, coriander seed, and cardamom, all in the same ale.[33] Modern brewers will be familiar with many of these spices—and many of us have included them in a beer or two. Other spices cited by Renfrow in recipes that pre-date 1700 include sage, mace, rosemary, thyme, sweet marjoram, mint, sweetbrier leaves, caraway seeds, hart's horn, anise, lemon peel, and "roasted oranges stuck with cloves."[34] Other historical recipes mention a combination of sweet gale, marsh rosemary, and either millfoil or yarrow in one recipe and in another, cardus benedictus, marjoram, betony, burnet, dried elderflower, thyme, pennyroyal, cardamom, and bayberries.[35]

While many of these herbs and spices are commonly seen in modern cooking, some have disappeared, often for good reason. Some were harmful, even fatal in significant quantities. Other additives were equally as bad. For example, in the late eighteenth century porter brewers added opium, tobacco, strychnine, and other noxious substances to their beers. If you run across an herb or spice or other possible additive that is new to you, be sure to check it out before putting it in a beer! As an aid to that, we include in chapter 3, where we discuss brown ale ingredients, comments on some of the more unusual herbs and spices used by pre-industrial brewers.

Industrial Brewing and Brown Ale

The first distinct and lasting beer style to emerge from the hodgepodge of brews being made in the early 1700s was porter. It began as a cocktail of three beers—pale ale, stale, and mild ale—designed to satisfy both the palate and the purse. The stale and mild were brown-colored ales. Some current authorities simply call them "brown ale," although it is not clear that anyone at the time used this term to describe these beers.

Legend credits Ralph Harwood with the creation of a distinct porter beer in 1722. Indeed, by 1726, consumption of a drink by that name was well recognized in London.[36] Most likely, the porter made by Harwood and the cocktail by the same name shared the title for some years. In addition, similar beers appear to have been offered under different names by different brewers. Only in retro-spect do people call all of these beers porter.

The popularity of porter-like beverages soared in the 1700s. With this mass consumption came mass produc-tion. By 1750, a handful of brewers were vying to be the biggest and fastest-growing porter producers. By the end of the century, tremendous capital had been invested in a small number of porter production plants and the world's first truly industrial beer ruled both in London and beyond.

During the century of porter's ascendancy and reign, the terms that brewers used to describe beer were rapidly evolving. Mathias provides this informative narrative:

> While Whitbread was certainly a porter brewer, only the word "mild beer" appeared in his books until a "New Porter Tun Room" was valued in 1760. The valuation of beer stocks in Thrale's brewery in 1748 included, besides the only important item of "mild beer" (the staple porter), stale beer, cloudy beer, eager beer (both these last being dete-riorated stock waiting to be "cured" in the autumn), good amber, stale, amber, brown

ale, brown small and pale small. Truman similarly, although not brewing brown ale, had amber and stout (brown, pale and "elder") in his 1741 *Rest Book*, although again mild beer was the only important item. Amber and pale brews (never significant in quantity from the 1740s) dropped out generally in the course of the next decades, when porter alone, of standard and "export" strengths, remained; that is, mild beer, stale beer, brown stout and pale stout.[37]

Here, for the first time, was a species of beer specifically called "brown ale" by its brewer. Coincidentally, there was a staggering array of other beer names—an indication of a rapidly developing sophistication about the differences between various sorts of brews.

The term *mild* particularly catches the eye, since mild and brown ales are closely related. Some brewers were using "mild" to describe products that, in retrospect, have been classified as porter. From what is known of dark milds today, it is not hard to imagine that a full-strength example would look a lot like a porter. In addition, small or common beer was produced in both pale and brown versions.

At about the same time that these brewers were making milds and brown ales, brown ale is mentioned in a brewing text. Corran says of the *London and Country Brewer*, first published in 1750: "The various types of beer on sale are enumerated—stout butt beer, strong brown ale, common brown ale, pale and amber ales and beers and small beer."[38]

Corran also gives another tie between porter and brown ale:

> The strong (first) extract of malt was still taken off to make strong beer, and successive worts drawn off for common ale or beer and finally for small beer, all from one charge of malt. Prices quoted are:

Stout Beer	1 bbl	30s
Stitch or Strong Brown Ale	1bbl, 1 firkin	21s 4d
Common Brown Ale	1.5 bbl	16s
Intire small beer	5–6 bbls	7s–8s[39]

The middle column of this chart gives the length, or quantity, of beer produced from one quarter (eight bushels) of malt. The first three would be produced from successive mashes of the same grist. At the conclusion of each mash, the liquid was runoff, but sparging was not employed. Corran notes that the intire was "brewed from all the malt and not just the last washings." Thus, the brewer apparently made *either* the first three brews *or* the larger batch of intire. The right-hand column gives the selling price per barrel.

Before porter came along, *stout* was simply a term for strong beer. During porter's reign, stout developed a specific meaning as "strong porter." In addition, intire was certainly a name for porter. As a result, this chart seems to indicate that in 1750 the same grist was used for producing porter, stout, and brown ale. The only difference between them was the OG of the brews.

The *London and Country Brewer* is also the first brewing text to identify differences in the malts used by brewers. Stopes reprinted numerous pages of this text in his work a century later, in particular the section entitled "Of the Nature and Use of Pale, Amber, and Brown Malts."[40] Here, it is apparent that brewers had different types of malt available. Their use, both alone and together in various combinations, probably helped generate the many varieties of beer evident during this period.

In its earliest days, porter was supposedly brewed from grists composed only of brown malt. But by the early

1800s, porter grists were more complex and often included pale, amber, and brown malts all together. The proportions of each malt varied widely, and some brewers dropped the pale or the amber malt entirely. Thus, we can only speculate about the exact composition of the grist that would have been used for making the combination of stout and brown ales or intire as noted in the *London and Country Brewer.*

The general confusion about the relationship between porter, stout, mild ale, and brown ale is complicated by the nomenclature of the day. The rise of porter as a beer for the masses resulted in specialization among brewers. Those who made porter and its relations came to be known as "brown beer brewers." Throughout the period from 1750 to about 1900, we find references to "brown beer" that mean porter and stout rather than some other variation on the theme. One such passage, from 1820, provides an example of this usage:

> Brown beer, or Porter, was introduced about 1720, chiefly on account of the aptitude of pale beer becoming stale. Brown beer was generally used among the labouring class of men, and indeed, from the strength it was

brewed, and the age it was kept, it was almost impossible for any but active and laborious people to drink and digest it.

As a result of this terminology, many references to "brown beer" can be found, but all of them lead right back to porter.

Beyond the specific citations given previously from the mid-1700s, we find no other references to a specific "brown ale" product prior to the twentieth century. Still, some interesting beers appear that may have served as models for later brown ales. One of the first comes from Burton-on-Trent around 1800. Although Burton is strongly connected with the creation of India pale ale and the brewing of pale beers in general, these developments did not come until a few years later. In 1791, the Baltic customers of a Burton brewer named Benjamin Wilson complained that his beers were "excessively dark in comparison to that of his rivals in the trade, evidently believing that paleness was a desirable quality."[41] This might lead one to think that the remaining Burton ales of the day were rather pale in color, were it not for Mathias's characterization of them: "The traditional Burton ale sent to the Baltic was reputedly 'nut-brown,' fairly sweet, and of great strength."[42] Thus, Wilson's ale must have been *quite* brown in order to prompt complaints. In addition, the Burton beers of this time had a complexion and balance rather like some brown ales of today.

Another brown-colored ale from this period comes from Dr. John Harrison and his colleagues at the Durden Park Beer Circle near London. They classify their collection of historical recipes according to color but list only six in the "brown" to "dark brown" range. Four of these are Scottish ales from the late nineteenth or early twentieth centuries. The remaining two come from early 1800s England and bear further examination.

The first of these was a 1.060 OG beer called Kingston Amber Ale. Harrison notes: "Amber ales were popular in London. Ratios of amber malt to pale malt varied from 3:1 to 1:1, OGs from 50 to 70 [1.050 to 1.070], and hop rates from three-eighths to three-quarters ounce per gallon. Amber ales are similar in style to Theakston's Old Peculiar."[43]

Although named "amber ale," the result of this recipe fits the general description of brown ale. The 1-gallon recipe calls for 2 ounces of chocolate malt in addition to 1.25 pounds each of pale and amber malt. Hopping is provided by three-quarters ounce of Fuggles or Goldings added at the beginning of the boil. Another text on brewing from 1822 also gives a recipe for amber ale. It mixes amber malt with pale malt in a ratio of three to one.[44]

The second beer from Harrison is Dorchester Ale, dated approximately 1800. A barley wine by today's reckoning, this 1.100-OG brew would have fallen well short of the strongest ales during its day. Harrison notes that the original used nothing but amber and brown malts to yield a dark brown ale. Using today's ingredients, his recipe for 1 gallon includes 1 pound pale malt, 2 pounds crystal malt, 1 pound brown malt, 8 ounces malt syrup, and 1.25 ounces Fuggles or Goldings hops added at the beginning of the boil.[45]

These recipes and others from the first two decades of the 1800s are not called brown ale, but they use the three known malts to yield beers that were brown in color. So, they were related to the brown ales of today, in spirit if not in name.

We Lose Our Story Line

In 1817, Daniel Wheeler invented the drum roaster and changed the course of beer history. He also severed what had been a close kinship between porter, stout, and brown ale.

Wheeler's roaster brought black malts to the brew house and black beers to the tavern. This ebony enlightenment drew a new line among the beers of color. Henceforth, some—namely porter and stout— would be associated with black malt and roasted barley; the others would not. One example of this is seen in the chronicles of a nineteenth-century brewer who denotes porter and stout brewed without Wheeler's patent malt as "brown beers" and those brewed with it as "black beers."[46]

At about this same time, pale ale began its ascent. By 1850, it had usurped porter's position as the number one beer of Britain. Although porter and stout would survive in a secondary role for many more years, the auxiliary brown beers would mostly disappear. Thus, for nearly a century brown ale made from malt was essentially unseen in Britain.

Despite this absence, we did find some brownish beverages made both in Britain and the United States during the nineteenth century. Most were weak common beers that relied on some combination of molasses and brown sugar for their fermentables. For balance, they commonly used hops, ginger, or spruce.

As an example from Britain, Renfrow provides a recipe for "Treacle-Beer, A Table Beer" dated 1829. It calls for three pounds molasses in six to eight gallons of water, plus a handful of hops, with the option to add a little ginger root.[47] A similar preparation from America's *Practical Housewife* (1860) calls for six pounds molasses plus eight to nine tablespoons spruce essence to make nine gallons of Brown Spruce Beer.[48]

While these "beers" bear little resemblance to the brown ales of today, they help to demonstrate the range of brown fermented beverages that have been produced in the past. They also provide another link to porter, which—prior to the advent of black malt—was sometimes colored with molasses.

The Twentieth Century

Between 1820 and 1920, brown ale as such appears to have been quite rare. However, its brother, mild ale, was often seen. Writing in *Brewing Techniques* magazine, mild man Dave Sutula gives details:

> As the practice of aging ales for a long period of time fell from popular use, so the term "brown ale" gradually fell from use and the term "mild ale" broadened to refer to an entire set of beers that were malty and brown

in color. References to mild ale are numerous between 1850 and 1900, and the products sold under that name fit into a wide spectrum of beers with gravities ranging from 1.055 to 1.080.[49]

This passage alludes to the original meaning of mild as a beer that was young and unaged. The early "cocktail" porters combined mild and aged brown beers plus pale ale. Thus, when porter production began, it was standard practice to age a portion of the beer for a year or more and then blend that with fresh beer before sending it out to pubs. (Perhaps the eighteenth-century brown ale was pure, aged porter!) The nineteenth-century pale ales did not use significant aging, so as Sutula says, aging began to disappear as a common brewing technique.

Thanks to black patent malt, brewers called their black beers either porter or stout. But the brown beers that remained needed a new name. Since they were unaged, mild seemed most suitable. In 1908, a leading U.S. brewer defined mild as follows: "Mild beers, whether ale, porter or stout, are called such as undergo no secondary fermentation, but are marketed about seven days after the principal fermentation is finished."[50]

Here, "mild" was sometimes applied to *any* beer that was sold fresh and unaged. Still the production of a specific style called mild ale was in progress.

Today, mild ale is a style distinct from brown ale, but the close relationship between the two can't be denied. In the twentieth century, brown ale emerged as a bottled product, and many authorities describe it simply as the bottled version of mild.[51] Indeed, Reg Drury, head brewer at Fuller's in London, says that the brown ale once marketed by the company was precisely that.[52] Most of the mild ale brewed was cask conditioned and served on draft. But a portion was filtered, primed with a substantial amount of sugar, and then bottled as brown ale.

Unfortunately, Fuller's stopped producing first the brown and then the mild due to lack of sales. Today, so few brown ales are made in Britain that they can no longer be called bottled milds. Today's products stand on their own as brown ales.

This illuminates the close relationship between mild and brown ales in the twentieth century. It allows us to revisit the milds of the late nineteenth and early twentieth centuries and get a glimpse of the brown ale culture from that period. Wahl and Henius show a London mild with an OG of 1.052 to 1.057 that included 0.8 to 1.25 pounds of hops per U.S. barrel. By comparison to 10 other beer styles given in the same chart, this is the lowest-hopped and lightest-gravity British beer of the time.[53]

A few years later, British brewing expert H. Lloyd Hind suggested grist compositions for two gravities of mild ale.[54] Both relied on dark-colored pale ale or mild ale malts as their base. The first, at 1.045 OG, also included crystal malt and brown malt, each at 2.8% of the grist, as well as "sugar" equal to 17.5% of the grist. The second, at 1.040 OG, used only the dark base malt, plus 6.5% "diamber" malt for color. This lighter-gravity recipe also included 20% sugar and 7% wheat malt. The diamber malt appears to be similar to Munich malt in that it has significant color but retains its diastatic power. The modest specialty malts used in these recipes may have left them somewhat pale, but their use to enhance the color and flavor of the beer continues in today's brown ales.

"The Dog" Fetches Brown Ale from Oblivion

By the time Hind was writing about brewing, today's best-known brown ale had already been born.

In 1924, Barras Ramsey, chairman of Scottish and Newcastle Breweries, was aware of the increasing demand for bottled beers. In response, his brewery's star young brewmaster and future chairman, Jim Porter, went to work.

Porter was born to a brewing family in Burton-on-Trent and grew up to study brewing at the university and later at Newcastle with Thomas Watson Lovibond—creator of the beer color scale. He became *Colonel* Jim Porter at the age of 27, commanding a battalion in World War I. As he settled into brewing again after the war, drinkers became interested in bottled beers.

Starting in 1924, Porter worked closely with the brewery's chief chemist, conducting experiments in brewing and blending to develop a product that would suit the bottled-beer market. Three years later, he had developed a deep amber-colored ale that he believed would do a good job of slaking the thirst of the hardworking locals. In 1927, Newcastle Brown Ale, or "Newkie Broon," was launched.

The following year, Newkie Broon won gold medals at the International Brewers' Exposition in London, securing its reputation and an enduring name for brown beers in the twentieth century. The bottle label was changed to include the medals, resulting in the label's enduring "figure eight" silhouette.

By all accounts, Porter's brown was a big success. In 1930, sales reportedly increased by 30%. Among Newcastle natives, it was considered something of a "national drink," and was highly sought after wherever they traveled. Eventually, Newkie Broon was packaged in cans to further expand the market. Riding this success, Porter soon found himself appointed to Newcastle's board of directors and, eventually, became its chairman.

Newkie Broon's popularity has continued to increase. Today, it is the largest-selling bottled beer in the United Kingdom. This popularity has led to another nickname for the beer in its local market: the Dog. Pubgoers in the Northeast often refer to their nightly trip to the pub as "going out to walk the dog." And because Newcastle Brown Ale is often the beer they are seeking, the company has launched a whole advertising campaign referring to its beer as "the Dog."

While Newcastle's brown has been the best-known example of its style, others have emerged. The Samuel Smith's brewery in Yorkshire was also winning awards for bottled beers in the period after the World War I. While its current brown ale is a relative youngster, with just a quarter century of commercial success, Samuel Smith's has brewed brown ales "a lot, lot longer," says the company.

Built in 1758, Samuel Smith's is still using its original well, tapping into an underground lake that provides

Burton-like hard water. Using a yeast that has more than a century of history at the brewery, it still ferments in Yorkshire squares made of gray slate. And, while Newcastle has followed the path of mergers and combinations to become part of a mammoth brewing enterprise, Samuel Smith's remains a small, independent company. Here, the words *old brewery* have an authentic, European definition—one measured in centuries, not in weeks. As a result, the beer they produce provides one of the most flavorful and unique examples of brown ale found anywhere.

As the popularity of bottled brown rose in the North of England, a similar trend was happening in the South. Brewers such as Fuller's that included a mild ale in its lineup started to bottle the mild, using the name *brown* on the label. The few examples of London-style brown ale found today still show this heritage, with a gravity and color derived from mild but a body and sweetness that betrays the often heavy sugar priming received before bottling.

With the resurgence of craftbrewing in the United States, where most brewpubs and many microbreweries produce their own versions of this smooth-drinking brew, brown ale is proving that every dog will have its day. Today, there are approximately 300 different brown ales from craftbrewers all over North America. A rare few match the parameters of the English styles, but most occupy new ground, as we will show in chapter 2.

We can't leave the history of brown ale without some mention of the American homebrewing movement of the late twentieth century. Homebrewers helped establish a distinct breed of brown ale in the early 1980s, when the organizers of the Dixie Cup Homebrew Competition began accepting entries in a style that came to be known as "Texas brown ale." This bold, highly hopped brown ale had the malt richness and brown color of an English brown ale but packed the bitterness, hop flavor, and aroma of hopped-up American pale ale.

In this chapter, we discussed beers that could be called brown ale. Along the way, we showed you quite a broad range of strengths, colors, and flavors. In chapter 2, we start to make some sense of it all by defining some common characteristics of modern brown ales.

CHAPTER 2

Brown Ale Profile: It's Brown, It's an Ale— Are We Going Too Fast for You?

When defining a beer style named for a color, one can follow either an easy path or a more difficult one. The easy path is to define the style by its color, to say, in this case, "Brown ale is any beer made with an ale yeast that is brown in color." End of chapter. Next question, please.

Surprisingly, this approach's biggest problem lies in defining the color brown. Both of the best-known English brown ales have a color of about 14 SRM (standard reference method). This value falls in the color ranges often defined for a number of other ale categories, including amber ale, India pale ale, best bitter, strong bitter, Scottish ale, and old ale. Thus, color alone cannot define this style.

To complicate matters further, the North American market generally sees only one style of imported brown ale, but the British typically recognize two distinct categories of brown ale: lighter, northern browns in the Newcastle tradition and darker, sweeter browns from around London.[1] It only seems fitting that we should detail the differences between these two styles while examining this subject.

Of course, we also analyze the distinct American variations of brown ale, since that is what many readers of this book will want to brew first. But in doing so, we run across a couple of American specialty beers based on brown ale, so we discuss those as well.

Thus, simplicity eludes us, but the resulting discussion should be interesting as well as illuminating.

English Brown Ales

The northern or Newcastle style is well known on this side of the pond. Commercial examples are Newcastle Brown Ale and Samuel Smith's Nut Brown Ale (known in its home country as strong brown ale). Both fall at the lighter end of the color range for brown ales and bring caramel and toasted malt flavors to the forefront of a well-balanced overall palate.

Northern-Style Brown Ales

Here are the basic parameters of the northern brown ale style:

> *Original specific gravity:* 1.045–50 (11.2–12.5 °Plato [°P])
>
> *Final gravity:* 1.008–14 (2–3.5 °P)
>
> *Alcohol:* 3.6–4% ABW; 4.5–5% ABV
>
> *Color:* 14–22 SRM
>
> *Bitterness:* 25–35 IBU (international bitterness units)

Most of us have likely tasted examples of these imported from England. In the bottle, they often suffer the ill effects of having been transported, but the draft products present a fairly consistent example of the profile. The English National Guild of Wine and Beer Judges defines the style as follows:

> **Newcastle Brown Ale [northern-style brown ale]:** The OG of 45 to 50 is reflected in an alcohol level of 4.5 to 5.0%. The color should be a light reddish brown and the

bouquet a blend of caramel and hop. The flavor should be a full bodied blend of caramelized malt with medium bitterness and noticeable sweetness.[2]

Commercial examples of the style include Vaux Double Maxim, in addition to the classics Newcastle Brown Ale and Samuel Smith's Nut Brown Ale. In the United States, several brewpubs and microbreweries produce a beer with a similar balance, such as Dunraven Ale from CooperSmith's Pub and Brewing in Fort Collins, Colorado, and the brown ale from Saint Arnolds in Houston, Texas.

Appearance: The northern-style brown ales occupy the lighter end of the brown ale range, with a deep amber to reddish light brown hue. They register around 14 to 16 SRM. In a pint glass at the pub, these beers easily pass for some of the darker American amber ales or perhaps an extra special bitter (ESB). Commercial examples are filtered brilliantly clear and, unlike cask milds, have a more pronounced carbonation level and head.

Aroma: Beers in this style offer a light, sweet malt aroma with toffee and caramel notes. A light but appealing fresh hop aroma may also be noticed, especially in the Samuel Smith's Nut Brown Ale. A light amount of fruity ester aroma can be evident in these beers, although it should not dominate. Diacetyl in low amounts may be evident.

Malt flavor: Caramel and toasted malt tones dominate the palate of this style. Most have a toffee-like note of sweetness as well as a toasted biscuit flavor from pale ale malt, mild ale malt, or a lightly toasted specialty malt such as Victory or Special Roast. A walnut-like nutty note is found in some. Most avoid the heavy, burnt toffee flavor of dark caramel as well as the burnt, ashen bitterness of roasted barley.

Hop bitterness/flavor: These beers display a moderate bitterness that balances the malt and lingers in the aftertaste. A slight hop flavor may be evident behind the malty sweetness on the palate.

Body/carbonation: These beers have a light to moderate body with moderate carbonation. They are not as fizzy as an American lager but are far more carbonated than an English real ale. A moderate carbonation "tickle" is evident on the tongue.

Finish/aftertaste: The northern browns finish slightly dry, compared to their southern counterparts. Newcastle shows a crisp finish with a slight, lingering hop bitterness, while Samuel Smith's finishes with both malt and bitter notes.

London-Style Brown Ales

The second category of English brown ale gets little recognition in North America. It includes darker, sweeter browns brewed in and around the vicinity of London. Because they are lower in alcohol content, they strongly resemble the dark milds still found in the Midlands and in the surrounding counties. Here are the basic parameters:

> *Original specific gravity:* 1.035–1.040
> (8.8–10 °Plato)
> *Final gravity:* 1.006–1.014 (1.5–3.5 °P)
> *Alcohol:* 2.8–3.2 ABW; 3.5–4 ABV
> *Color:* 20–35 SRM
> *Bitterness:* 12–20 IBU

Many sources cite Mann's Brown Ale from Britain as the prototype of this style, but it is not imported into the United States. Here, we get an example called Cobnut Nut Brown Ale from the Tollemache and Cobbold brewery in Suffolk, England. Despite the *nut brown* name, it is opaquely dark and deeply malty. Finally, some American products approach the same basic flavor profile in a higher-gravity beer, including Oregon Nut Brown and Oasis Tut Brown Ale.

The English National Guild of Wine and Beer Judges defines the style as follows:

> **London Brown Ale**: OG should be 35 to 40, giving an alcohol level of 3.5 to 4.0%. Color may vary from light to dark brown. The bouquet is malty backed by caramel. The beer should be sweet on the palate, giving a smooth blend of malt and caramel with low hop flavor.[3]

Fuller's brewery in London once made such a beer, with an OG of 1.033 (8.3 °P) and a color of 90 to 100 EBC (46 to 51 SRM). Although this pre-fermentation OG is a bit low for the style, a full one-half gallon of priming sugar was added to each barrel at bottling, so the effective OG would have been well into the appropriate range.

Appearance: These beers are very deep copper to very brown in color and often opaque, showing a higher proportion of more high-color caramel malt in the 90 to 120 °Lovibond (°L) range, along with increased proportions of chocolate malt. They are usually filtered clear with less head than the northern browns.

Aroma: Southern browns have a rich, sweet toffee aroma from the caramel malt. Fruity esters, such as plum and raisin, may be evident. Hop aroma is very faint, if noticeable at all. Diacetyl may be very slightly evident.

Malt flavor: In some cases, substantial portions of dark caramel malts give these beers a sweet, deep caramel-like flavor that many beer lovers describe as "luscious." Others get their hue mostly from caramel coloring and dark sugar and may have a more pedestrian malt flavor. Those display a pronounced fruitiness. There is little or no perceivable roasty or bitter black malt flavor.

Hop bitterness/flavor: Hop bitterness and flavor are extremely low.

Body/carbonation: These beers tend to be fuller in body and lower in carbonation than the northern versions.

Finish/aftertaste: The finish of these beers is definitely on the sweet side with a smooth, malty aftertaste.

In this style, one can clearly see the close relationship between mild ale and brown ale discussed in chapter 1.

American Brown Ales

An odd flip-flop between mild and brown ales occurs somewhere over the Atlantic. In Britain, mild ales—although declining in popularity—still issue from dozens of breweries. Brown ales on the other hand are difficult to find beyond the well-known few.

In the United States, the situation is reversed. Beer enthusiasts can find more than 300 brown ales from brewpubs and microbreweries around the country. When it comes to mild ales, however, the search is literally ten times more difficult—fewer than three dozen breweries make this style.

American homebrewers and craftbrewers, inspired at least in part by the classic English examples discussed previously, have created their own interpretations of brown ale. Still, we find dichotomies even here.

Lured by opportunity, many early homebrewers piled lots of everything into their beers: specialty malts that provided color and flavor complexity and good American hops that delivered assertive hop flavors and aromas. These beers didn't fit the English brown ale style, so an American brown category was created. It called for lots of hops and all-malt grain bills with robust starting gravities. The movement toward these hoppy brown ales was first recognized in Texas (although Californians claim that distinction as well).

Eventually, the high-hop criteria were recognized as part of the national guidelines. For example, the rules and regulations for the 1992 National Homebrew Competition stated that American brown ales should have "high hop bitterness, flavor and aroma."[4] As a result, many homebrewers have produced brown ales that have a very assertive hop profile.

While some American-made commercial brown ales have followed this lead, it appears that most have taken a different path. A random sampling of commercial products shows far less assertive bitterness, while taste tests demonstrate more subdued hopping in the flavor and aroma. A close look at key values for various categories of brown ale also indicates divergence, as shown in table 1.

TABLE 1

British versus American Brown Ales

	Commercial Browns from England[a]	Homebrewed English Style[a]	Commercial Browns from United States	Homebrewed American Style[a]
BU:GU ratio	0.580	0.540	0.510	0.950
Original gravity	1.046	1.055	1.053	1.051
Percent British hops	100	55	25	2

[a]Data from Ray Daniels, *Designing Great Beers: The Ultimate Guide to Brewing Classic Beer Styles* (Boulder, Colo.: Brewers Publications, 1996), 220–227.

The key value here is the BU:GU ratio—a strong indicator of the overall balance between malt and hops. The BU:GU ratio is a tool used extensively in *Designing Great*

Beers to describe the balance between malt and hops. It is represented as a single number with a value generally between 0.25 (very malty) to 1 (very bitter). The BU portion is based upon the international bittering units (IBU) contained in the beer. GU is the OG of the beer (in SG) minus 1 times 1,000. The brown ales made by American commercial brewers show the same approximate value as those for commercial brown ales from England and homebrewed English-style brown ales from the United States. In essence, the current American commercial interpretation of brown ale splits the difference between the hop-dominated American brown ale popular with homebrewers and the malt-balanced northern-style brown ales of England. The gravity and hop varieties are largely American, but the balance follows more of an English approach.

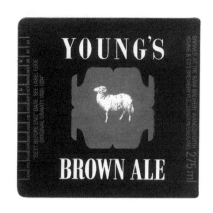

This observation fits well with many brewers' views of their brown ales. Several craftbrewers consider their brown ales as a natural antidote to a highly hopped flagship pale

ale. Not everyone likes a big hop flavor, and the brewers look to their browns to offer a malty, full-flavored alternative. "The brown is usually the favorite beer during tours," said Brock Wagner from Saint Arnold's in Houston, Texas. "People are afraid to buy a product called brown ale, but when they taste it, they like it."

Because the Association of Brewers (AOB) tries to maintain the same style guidelines for homebrewed beer and commercially brewed beer competitions, it can't really accommodate a divergence in style definitions between the two arenas. In recent years, its description of American brown ale has been softened to reflect commercial practice. In 1997, the statement on hops was "evident hop aroma and increased bitterness [over English brown ales]."[5] Despite this change in language, the quantitative values for the style didn't change. The following basic parameters still apply:

> *Original gravity:* 1.040–1.055 (10–13.5 °P)
> *Color:* 15–22 SRM
> *Bitterness:* 25–60 IBU

The AOB is not alone in this. The *1998 Style Guidelines* from the Beer Judge Certification Program use the exact same quantitative criteria, with a description that calls only for "higher alcohol and hop bittering levels."

Based on the random sample of commercial brown ales on which we collected quantitative data, *more than 90% of the beers fell outside these parameters.* Many showed lower bitterness levels, generally in the range from 20 to 24 IBUs. Several others had deeper color, ranging from 25 to 42 SRM. A few even went beyond the high end of the OG range, up to 1.070 (17.3 °P). The range of values is shown in table 2.

TABLE 2

Values for Commercial American Brown Ales

	IBU	OG (SG)	OG (°P)	BU:GU	SRM
Average	28	1.053	13.3	0.51	37
Minimum	20	1.045	11.3	0.40	26
Maximum	58	1.070	17.3	0.83	42

Source: Reprinted, by permission, from Ray Daniels, *Designing Great Beers: The Ultimate Guide to Brewing Classic Beer Styles* (Boulder, Colo.: Brewers Publications, 1996), 220–227.

Faced with this mismatch, one wonders if American brewers are simply making English brown ales with American hops. More directly, how do the commercial American brown ales fit the style criteria for English browns? Not too well, as it turns out. Only about a third of them fall into the English brown box. Gravity and color are the main things that knock them out—only one or two are over-hopped.

If commercial practice dictates style parameters, then clearly American brown ale needs a new set of values. We discuss these next.

American Brown Ales

The following guidelines seem to describe the majority of the brown ales sold in America today:

> *Original specific gravity:* 1.045–1.060 (11.3–14.8 °P)
> *Final gravity:* 1.010–1.016 (2.5–4 °P)
> *Alcohol:* 3.5–5 ABW; 4.3–6.2 ABV
> *Color:* 18–45 SRM
> *Bitterness:* 20–40 IBU

Description: This style is light to dark brown and has medium to medium-full body. Hop character may vary from light to assertive in aroma and flavor. Hop character may come from American, English, or "noble-type" varieties. There are low to moderate esters, little or no diacetyl, and medium to high maltiness in aroma and flavor. Also present is a medium bitterness with an aftertaste that carries both malt and hops.

Brewers who want to retain the old assertively hopped interpretation might do so under one of its original names: Texas brown ale. The guidelines for that might look as shown in the next subsection.

Texas Brown Ales

Original specific gravity: 1.045–1.055 (11.3–13.5 °P)
Final gravity: 1.010–1.018 (2.5–4.5 °P)
Alcohol: 3.3–4.7 ABW; 4.1–5.9 ABV
Color: 14–30 SRM
Bitterness: 30–60 IBU

Description: This style is amber to brown and has medium to medium-full body. The high hop aroma, flavor, and bitterness are provided by American hop varieties. There is medium to high maltiness in aroma and flavor, low esters, and no diacetyl. After-taste is distinctly bitter, but some lingering malt character is possible.

Some might argue that our distinction between Texas and American brown ales puts too fine a point on the issue. Despite this, we see real differences here, differences that are at least as great as those currently being drawn between pale ale and amber ale or brown porter and robust porter.

American Specialty Brown Ales

In addition to brown ales made with traditional ingredients, American brewers make a number of specialty beers built on the brown ale base. Since history has shown that everything from spices to spruce and molasses to maize have found their way into brown ales in the past, we take a look at the broad category of specialty brown beers. Their basic parameters are as follows:

Original specific gravity: 1.040–1.065 (10–16 °P)
Final gravity: 1.010–1.018 (2.5–4.5 °P)
Alcohol: 3.3–6 ABW; 4.2–6.5 ABV
Color: 15–45 SRM
Bitterness: 20–60 IBU

Clearly, these beers can be all over the map in terms of color, gravity, and bitterness. Brown ale's popularity in American brewpubs and with small craftbrewers has made it a perfect canvas for many of the more creative brewers to dabble in extreme forms of self expression.

To spice up their brown ales, brewers are adding everything from additional sugars (Tommyknocker Maple Nut Brown) to flavorings (Rogue Hazelnut Brown Nectar) to fruit (Odell's Merry Berry Brown). And speaking of spice, brown ales are often the base beers when brewers concoct their annual holiday spiced wassails.

Obviously, it would be pure folly to try to list all of the aroma and flavor characteristics of this wide range of beers. Instead, we will describe some of the characteristics added by the various adjuncts brewers use in these specialty browns.

Sugars

Maple syrup, added most often postprimary fermentation, imparts a light, nutty sweetness to the nose and a rich sweetness to the flavor. It also adds fermentable sugar.

Molasses, added most often during the boil or in the fermenter, adds color and sweetness, as well as its own distinct flavor.

Honey, if added in the boil, will contribute a little flavor and sweetness, but it will primarily add to the beer's alcohol because the boil drives off flavor-producing aromatic compounds. Added postboil to the hot wort or pasteurized and put in the fermenter, it adds a distinct honey flavor as well as some sweetness.

Fruit

Brewers have experimented with many fruits in brown ales, from raspberries and cherries to black currants. A tarter fruit, to balance the caramel malt sweetness, usually works best.

Nut Extracts

Hazelnut extract has become a popular additive for brown ales, contributing a sweet, almost chocolate-like flavor and aroma.

Herbs and Spices

The herbs and spices that have been—and might be—used in brown ale are described in chapter 3.

Like most beer styles, brown ale shows considerable diversity. Further, the small number of examples in Britain and the evolving nature of the American craftbrew market mean that the style will probably continue to change. Whether you brew just one or brew them all, you can enjoy the style and share it with others to help influence the direction the style takes.

CHAPTER 3

Brewing Brown Ales

In making brown ale, brewers have considerable room for variation and experimentation. A fine brown ale can be made just as easily by the novice extract-based homebrewer as by the seasoned all-grain professional. This chapter examines the key ingredients of brown ale—including malt, hops, yeast, and water—and the essential issues to consider in selecting them.

Malt

The key ingredient of brown ale is malt. If you look at brewing a beer as being somewhat like making a stew, malt would be the meat of your recipe. It provides essential sugar for the wort, as well as much of the beer's character as evidenced by the color, flavor, and body of the finished beer.

The malt character for brown ale comes from two sources: pre-packaged malt extract (either liquid or dry) or a mash of grains selected by the brewer. While many readers will confine themselves to the all-grain approach, excellent brown ales can be made using extract, so let us consider how it should be employed.

Malt Extract

Malt extract brings convenience at the expense of flavor and control. It's much easier and faster to open a package of extract than to conduct a full mash. But the wort and subsequent beer that result from an all-extract approach may be unpredictable in gravity, fermentability, and flavor.

To overcome these shortcomings, you need to follow two simple guidelines. First, some portion of grain should always be used in formulating your brown ale. Second, your extracts should be carefully selected to yield the results you desire.

The use of grain with extract can be accomplished in several ways, but it need not be complicated. For example, most homebrewers use a grain bag to steep a pound or so of specialty grains in the brewing water before the malt extract is added. This is a perfectly valid and useful technique. As a slightly more advanced step, those with a modest mashing capability may combine the specialty grains with a pound or so of base malt (pale ale malt) to perform a mini-mash that will then be supplemented with extract during the boil.

Many excellent and award-winning beers have been made using these techniques. Furthermore, any all-grain recipe can be converted to a grain-extract recipe by substituting an appropriate amount of pale extract for the pale malt. Simply use about half a pound of dry extract or two-thirds pound of syrup for each pound of grain replaced.

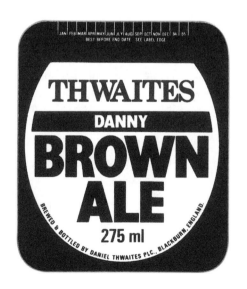

The use of grains in your recipe addresses the issue of flavor to a great extent. Still, you must use care in selecting your extract. You should limit your use of extract to the unhopped,

light- or pale-colored products, as these generally provide the best results. But even these products vary in many ways, such as with their flavor, specific gravity, and fermentability.

The flavor of extracts varies widely. The best have a pleasant pale malt flavor that is similar to that of pale malt. Others provide a caramel flavor that is more like crystal malt. The least desirable provide very little malt flavor and may carry some undesirable characteristics, such as a tinny or ink-like flavor. The flavor is best judged by making a small amount of beer (one quart or so) with no hops and fermenting it with your standard yeast. Side-by-side comparisons of several brands can also be informative.

Dry extracts generally provide a predictable amount of gravity to your brew, but with liquid extracts, this is not always the case. The standard here is the gravity produced when one pound of extract is dissolved in one gallon of water. Dry extracts generally produce a wort of about 1.045 specific gravity (SG), while liquid extracts average about 1.036 SG. Recent data, however, has

TABLE 3

Fermentability of Popular Malt Extracts

Brand	Fermentability (%)
Laaglander Dried (Light)	44.4
Northwestern (Dry, Gold)	57.1
Munton & Fisons Light Syrup	57.5
Munton & Fisons Spray-Dried (Light)	59.5
John Bull Unhopped Light Syrup	60.4
Alexander's Pale Syrup	61.9
Northwestern Syrup (Gold)	61.8
Coopers Unhopped Light Syrup	64.1

Source: Reprinted, by permission, from Ray Daniels, *Designing Great Beers: The Ultimate Guide to Brewing Classic Beer Styles* (Boulder, Colo.: Brewers Publications, 1996), 15.

shown that with liquid extracts this number may drop to as low as 1.028 SG, so you should be prepared for variation until you are very familiar with a particular brand of extract.

By paying attention to the fermentability of the malt extract used, you can vary the body of your finished beer to achieve an effect appropriate to the style being brewed. Most extracts show an apparent fermentability of 57 to 62%. Those with lower fermentability will be fuller bodied; those with greater fermentability will be thinner. Table 3 shows some values for the fermentability of some popular light malt extracts. The best course is to experiment with a few extracts to find those that work best for you.

CHARLES WELLS

WELCOME
BROWN ALE
275 ml   9.68 fl oz
BREWED & BOTTLED IN ENGLAND
BY CHARLES WELLS LTD. AT BEDFORD

Base Malt

As with most ales, the grist for brown ale consists mainly of pale ale malt or a similar substitute. In both Britain and America, brewers generally prefer two-row malt for the making of brown ales. In America, this base malt product is often simply called two-row malt. It is a utilitarian grain that small-scale brewers use in making both ales and lagers of all hues. In Britain, as well as among some American craftbrewers, the more specialized pale ale malt is used as the base for these recipes. While general, two-row malts are kilned at temperatures up to 185 °F (85 °C), pale ale malts kiln-out at temperatures of up to 200 °F (95 °C), thereby resulting in an increase in both color and toasted-malt flavor.

While professional brewers will generally be constrained to a single base malt for all of their recipes (or at least all of their ale recipes), homebrewers have the freedom to select and experiment widely. Table 4 shows the color values of some of the malts that might be suitable as the base for a brown ale recipe. Included

TABLE 4

Color Values of Selected Base Malts

General Two-Row Malts	Color (SRM)
Schreier Two-Row Pale	1.4–2.0
Minnesota Malting Co. Two-Row Pale	1.4–2.0
Briess Two-Row Brewers Malt	1.5–2.0
Gambrinus Pale	1.8–2.0
Great Western Premium Two-Row	1.8–2.1

Pale Ale Malts	Color (SRM)
Muntons Pale	2.0–3.0
Baird British Pale Ale	2.0–3.0
Beeston Best Halcyon Pale Ale	2.2
Beeston Best Maris Otter Pale Ale	2.3
Beeston Best Pipkin Pale Ale	2.3
Beeston Golden Promise	2.7
Gambrinus ESB Pale	3.0
Pauls Pale Ale	2.5–3.5
Crisp English Pale Ale	2.8–3.5
DeWolf-Cosyns Pale Ale	2.7–3.8

Pale Ale Malts	Color (SRM)
Crisp Maris Otter	3.4
Briess Pale Ale	3.2–3.6
Great Western Northwest Ale	3.0–4.0
Schreier Special Pale	3.2–3.8

Mild Ale Malts	Color (SRM)
Pauls Best Mild Ale	3.5–4.5
Muntons Mild Ale	4.0

Source: Data from "1997 Brewers' Market Guide," *Brewing Techniques*: 98–101.

in this list are two mild ale malts from Britain. Mild ale malts kiln-out at up to 220 °F (105 °C) for an even higher color than pale ale malts. They are typically used in the production of brown ale's little brother, dark mild ale. For those with the flexibility to do so, the use of mild ale malt in making a brown ale would be an excellent experiment.

Specialty Malts

The distinctive character of brown ale comes from that smaller portion of the grist (usually 10 to 20% of the total) composed of specialty malts. These malts provide both the deep color and the complex malt flavor of the beer. In creating a brown ale recipe, brewers can select from a wide variety of different specialty malts. In practice, however, some clear patterns seem to define both British and American styles.

First, nearly all recipes include a good portion of crystal malt—generally accounting for 8 to 13% of the grist. This adds body, caramel flavor, color, and malt complexity to the beer.

Second, most recipes add a small portion of chocolate malt or another deeply roasted grain to account for about 2 to 3% of the grist. This deepens the color and adds a roasted and sometimes burnt flavor component to the beer.

TABLE 5

**Incidence and Proportion of
Specialty Malts in Commercial American Brown Ales**

	Incidence	PROPORTION		
		Average	Minimum	Maximum
Crystal	100%	13%	6%	29%
Chocolate	75%	2%	1%	5%
CaraPils	50%	5%	3%	7%
Munich	50%	10%	5%	19%
Other[a]	50%	9%	3%	14%
Roasted	33%	1%	1%	2%
Wheat	33%	9%	5%	15%
Black	8%	4%	4%	4%

[a]Other includes aromatic, biscuit, brown, Special "B," and Victory malts.

TABLE 6

**Incidence and Proportion of
Specialty Fermentables in Commercial British Mild Ales**

	Incidence	Proportion
Crystal	71%	8%
Fermentables	53%	12%
Chocolate	28%	6%
Wheat	28%	5%
Black	25%	5%
Roasted	19%	6%
Corn	18%	11%

Tables 5 and 6 list the incidence and proportion of specialty malts in commercial American brown ales and British mild ales.

Beyond the common components of crystal and chocolate malt, brown ales may contain any of many other specialty malts. Each is added according to the brewer's tastes to help build the complexity of the malt profile by adding new flavors to the beer. The remainder of this section discusses selection of specialty malts for brown ales.

Crystal Malts

Despite the uniform use of crystal malt, nearly every brewer can exert some judgment and variation in selecting theirs. Nearly every maltster makes crystal malt, and most produce it in different grades or colors. As a result, most brewers can select from among a score or more of crystal malts, each with a distinct flavor contribution. For increased complexity, crystal malts from two or more maltsters can be mixed in a single recipe.

The color of crystal malt plays a role in determining the amount that is used, but most brewers stay in the 8 to 13% range, as shown in tables 5 and 6. English brewers—who may rely on caramel coloring to enhance the appearance of their beer—tend to use smaller quantities, 8% on average. American brewers use more, ranging from 6 to 29%.

Crystal or caramel malts provide the distinctive sweet flavor and amber-to-brown color most often associated with brown ales. In his *World Guide to Beer*, Michael Jackson refers to the character of these grains as "luscious." Making them involves steeping or stewing green malt at temperatures of around 150 °F (66 °C). This allows the enzymes to convert the starches to sugar, in effect mashing the grain and giving a liquefied sugary center within the grain husk. The kilning room is then ventilated and the temperature raised to dry the center into a hard, caramelized core not unlike rock candy. Depending on the time and temperature used for drying, crystal malts may range from a color of about 20 °L to greater than 120 °L.

The light caramel malts (30 to 40 °L) add a light caramel color and a toffee-like or biscuity flavor and aroma. Medium caramel malts (50 to 80 °L) produce an amber to reddish hue and impart a rich caramel sweetness and aroma that some brewers refer to as plum- or raisin-like. Dark caramel malts (90 to 120 °L) deliver an intense reddish-brown color. The aroma can be like burnt toffee, and the flavor almost bittersweet.

For English brown ales, these malts should not make up more than 10% of the grist, at the risk of adding excess bitterness.

A distinctive malt called Special "B" comes from the DeWolf-Cosyns Maltings in Belgium. It has a deep reddish brown color (100 °L) and imparts a rich, fruity flavor and aroma not unlike plums or raisins. It is commonly used in Belgian brown ales and can add complexity to any brown ale when used in small portions.

Roasted Malts

When it comes to the darkest grains, most maltsters offer several choices. In general, one must choose between chocolate malt, black patent malt, or roasted barley.

For brewing brown ales, chocolate malt is the most common selection. Its color ranges from 200 °L to over 500 °L, with flavors that go from a light milk chocolate to burnt coffee. A very small amount of chocolate malt goes a long way in a brown ale. For example, Pete's Wicked Ale contains only 1% chocolate malt, while most other recipes are limited to no more than 3%. On average, American brewers use chocolate for 2% of the grist, although some use as much as 5%. British brewers—having been more conservative with the crystal malt—use larger proportions of deeply colored malts, with chocolate malt averaging 6% when the recipe calls for it.

The highly roasted black malts range in color from 400 °L to more than 700 °L. Often they go by the name black patent, referring to the patented process that initially produced such malts. They contribute more sharp malt bitterness than do chocolate malts and—among American brewers—are generally employed in proportions of only 4% or so for brown ales. British brewers go a bit heavier, averaging 5% of the grist, when it is used.

Roasted barley is sometimes an ingredient in brown ale, although most brewers prefer to use crystal and chocolate instead. Roasted barley tends to darken the foam of the beer and contributes an acrid burnt flavor that may be viewed as inappropriate in this style. As a result, American brewers use it sparingly, 1% or so. In keeping with the pattern shown so far, British brewers are willing to add more, averaging 6% when used.

Roasting Your Own Amber and Brown Malts

Some of the malts that were once used to make brown ale are now difficult to find or are completely unavailable. To emulate eighteenth- and nineteenth-century recipes, you can roast your own malts according to the following procedures from Dr. John Harrison and the Durden Park Beer Circle.[a]

Procedure for Amber Malt

1. Place pale ale malt to a depth of one-half inch in a foil-lined cooking pan. Retain a few kernels in a separate plate to use for comparison during roasting.
2. Cook in an oven for 45 minutes at 230 °F and then for 20 to 60 minutes at 300 °F.
3. After the first 20 minutes at 300 °F, cut several kernels in half to inspect the color of the starchy endosperm. For amber malt, the endosperm should be "light buff" in color when finished. Continue heating at 300 °F until this color is achieved, usually 45 to 50 minutes.

Procedure for Brown Malt

Follow the procedure for amber malt. After the proper endosperm color is achieved, raise the oven temperature to 350 °F and continue heating until the endosperm is a "full buff" or "about the color of the paler types of brown wrapping paper."

Alternative Procedure

As an alternative to the previous two procedures, Randy Mosher[b] recommends filling a pan to a depth of no more than one inch and then heating the kernels as follows: 350 °F for 20 to 30 minutes for amber malt and 450 °F for 30 to 40 minutes for brown malt.

As with the previous two procedures, evaluate the extent of roasting by periodically examining a cross section of several kernels.

[a] J. Harrison, et al., *An Introduction to Old British Beers and How to Make Them*, 2d. ed. (The Durden Park Beer Circle, 1991), 4.

[b] Randy Mosher, *The Brewer's Companion*, revised (Seattle: Alephenalia Publications, 1996), 135.

Other Alternatives

For those with a hankering to explore history, brown and amber malts can still be found from certain maltsters, such as Crisp Malting Group and Beeston Malting Company. Commercially produced brown malt is dried for a short period at about 180 °C (390 °F), giving it a dark color (50 to 100 °L) and a deep toasty flavor. The flavor is described by one maltster as "very bitter, burnt."

Amber malt, with a color of about 20 to 50 °L, is both lighter in color and less assertive in flavor. Product literature describes it as having a "warm, pleasant, biscuit flavor with coffee undertones."

If you cannot find amber or brown malt, you can make your own following the procedures given in the sidebar, "Roasting Your Own Amber and Brown Malts" on pages 70 and 71.

Munich malt may seem like a strange choice for an English-bred ale style, but this German specialty adds an interesting flavor dimension. Munich malt is "high-dried," that is, kilned at temperatures similar to those used for making mild ale malt. It is slightly darker (5 to 10 °L) but retains enough enzyme power to be used as a base malt. For brown ales, this malt adds a drier, toasty malt flavor. When American brewers use it, it constitutes 10% of the grist on average but may range from 5 to 19%. British brewers' formulations don't include Munich malt. This is logical, since mild ale malt would probably be easier and less expensive to acquire.

Other choices of malts for brown ale include the full spectrum of lightly toasted malts with names such as biscuit and special roast. These malts contribute flavors and aromas ranging from freshly baked bread to a toasted English muffin. Specific malts that the American brewers we polled have included in brown ale recipes include aromatic, biscuit, and Victory.

The final constituents that often find a home in American-made brown ales are wheat and dextrin, or CaraPils malt. These two components help to enhance body and head retention without contributing much flavor. CaraPils is most often used, appearing in half of the recipes we examined and generally constituting about 5% of the grist. Wheat appeared in a third of the recipes and accounted for 9% of the grist on average.

Other Grains

Various adjunct grains are employed in small amounts by some brown ale brewers. In Britain, corn—in various forms—is sometimes used to lighten the body and flavor of beers. It is cooked separately in a cereal cooker and then added to the mash. Scottish and Newcastle Breweries use a percentage of corn in their Newcastle Brown Ale.

Other British brewers use *torrified wheat* in their ales. Torrified grains are heated until they puff like popcorn, similar in concept to the blown malt mentioned in some historic brewing texts. Torrified wheat adds mouthfeel and assists in head formation and retention. In America, wheat malt and torrified wheat are used to build better head retention.

Also, as mentioned in chapter 1, early brewers often used a high proportion of oats in their beer. Today, some brewers add flaked oats to contribute a richer, smoother mouthfeel to brown ales.

Hops

Depending on the brown ale style you choose to make, the hops may play either a starring role or a supporting one. In either case, proper selection and use of the hops are required to achieve the desired final beer character.

British brewers generally use English hop varieties in all of their ales, and the browns are no exception. When commercial mild ale recipes are used as a guideline, the four most popular varieties are Fuggles, Goldings, Challenger, and Northdown.[1] Some British brewers believe these versatile varieties can be used in any phase of the boil and will produce attractive features in bitterness, flavor, or aroma characteristics. Most, however, regard East Kent Goldings as the finest English aroma hop, with Fuggles as a commendable second. Challenger and Northdown also produce attractive flavor and aroma characteristics, but they are more often seen in bittering roles. American brewers might select hops from England, America, or even Germany. More than a quarter of all brown ale hop additions are made with English varieties or the direct American descendent, Willamette. (See table 7. East Kent Goldings and Willamette top this list.)

In making American-style browns, brewers generally prefer American hop varieties. The three Cs—Cascade, Chinook, and Centennial—get a lot of play among both professional brewers and homebrewers who produce the Texas brown style. These hop varieties produce the

TABLE 7

**Incidence of Hops by Variety
in American Commercial Brown Ales**

Type	Count
Cascade	6
Willamette	3
"American Varieties"	3
East Kent Goldings	2
Fuggles	2
Liberty	2
Northern Brewer	2
Perle	2
Brewers Gold	1
Centennial	1
Chinook	1
Mt. Hood	1
Northdown	1
Nugget	1
Tettnang	1
Total	29

distinct spicy, resinous, citrus characteristics associated with American craftbrewed beers. Among them, Cascade is used most often in flavor and aroma roles, but Centennial, with its medium alpha-acid content, has gained some popularity. Even the high-alpha Chinook is sometimes seen in late-boil additions.

Finally, some brewers add a pleasant but delicate hop aroma to their brown ales with German "noble-type" hops or their American cousins. We have seen Tettnang and Saaz employed. Table 7 shows the use of two Hallertau clones: Liberty and Mt. Hood.

Determining Hop Quantities

The recipes given in this book provide basic guidelines for hopping—suggesting not only hop variety, but also quantity. The amounts given are based on our own experiences at the time we brewed the individual beers. For those who want a more precise guideline for hopping, the estimated total bitterness for each recipe is also given.

Every brewery utilizes hops differently, thereby producing variations in bitterness, flavor, and aroma, even when the exact same protocol is followed. In addition, the actual level of bitterness, flavor, and aroma compounds found in a hop variety differs widely, even within the same year and same region of the country. As a result, making beer that possesses the hop character you desire requires both some art and some science.

The art comes into play in the flavor and aroma areas. Brewers develop both experience and preference on how each hop will contribute to the final flavor and aroma of their beers. That, combined with the basic recommendations provided by the recipes, will guide your final hop schedule.

The science can be of greatest use in hitting the target bitterness for each beer. Brewers who know—or want to learn—their own utilization levels can adjust each recipe to more closely match the recommended bitterness level. All this takes is knowing the alpha-acid content of the hops, along with the IBU calculation formulas given in appendix 1. This approach is also useful for those brewers who want to formulate their own recipes based on the guidelines given in chapter 2. Note that in both cases, you should begin by determining the quantities of aroma hops needed and then working backwards, fixing the quantity of bittering hops so that total bitterness will be approximately equal to the targeted value. (See appendix 1 for relevant formulas.)

Notes on Hop Varieties

In this section, we offer additional information about the major hop varieties that are often used for brewing brown ale.

Brewers Gold is a slightly hardier sibling of Bullion, also developed in England. It ranges from 5.5 to 8.5% alpha and has a spicier, fruitier flavor and aroma than Bullion. Many English brewers reject Brewers Gold as "too American," but it is the aroma hop used in Pete's Wicked Ale.

Bullion was developed in England in the 1930s and was once popular in the North American Pacific Northwest. It does not store well, however, so its popularity has waned. A mid- to high-alpha hop (6 to 9%), it imparts a smooth bitterness. When fresh, it is a good choice for bittering. It is not recommended for use as a flavor or aroma hop.

Cascade is a staple of American craftbrewers. A West Coast favorite, it has a very flowery, citrusy, grapefruit-like flavor and aroma. It is generally a fairly low-alpha hop (4 to 6%), but recent crops have reached alpha levels of up to 8%.

Centennial has gained a very loyal following in the short time since its 1990 debut. Bred as a mid- to high-alpha (10 to 12%) bittering hop, it has a citrusy flavor and aroma. It has become a favorite of West Coast brewers, who like its distinctive character.

Challenger is a good all-purpose English hop in the mid-alpha range (6.5 to 9%). It imparts a fruity, floral aroma and flavor with light spicy notes and sometimes yields an orange-like flavor. This combination of characteristics gives this hop a dual-use reputation.

Chinook has a distinctive piney and resinous flavor, even when boiled for an hour. As a higher-alpha hop (12 to 14%), it is best for bittering of Texas-style brown ales.

Columbus is a fairly new high-alpha (14 to 16%) bittering hop that has quickly won wide acceptance. If used later in the boil, it imparts a grassy note.

First Gold is a new dwarf variety of hop. Its flavor and aroma resemble Goldings, only with more spicy notes. With an alpha range of 6.5 to 8.5%, it produces a smooth, clean bitterness that makes it ideal for brown ales.

Fuggles is the other classic English flavor and aroma variety. It has a low alpha-acid content (4 to 5.5%) and an herbal, somewhat earthy flavor and aroma. Fuggles doesn't impart as much sweetness as Goldings. Like Goldings, it can be used for bittering, provided you use plenty of it.

Galena, introduced in the 1970s, is a moderately high-alpha (12 to 14%) hop and is hardier and overall more favorable than Bullion and Brewers Gold. It produces a clean bitterness, and its flavor and aroma are pleasantly floral.

Goldings is not a single variety, but a whole family of hops. Each is often named for its place of origin. East

Kent Goldings, from the English county of the same name, is the grand-daddy of the variety and is the signature hop in many English ales. This resiny, low-alpha (4 to 4.5%) hop imparts a light, smooth bitterness and a spicy, almost sweet flavor and aroma. Other Goldings varieties are grown in British Colum-bia, Oregon, Washing-

ton, and even Slovenia. All have similar alpha-acid ranges, except for Oregon Goldings, which runs a bit higher (5 to 6%). The Oregon Goldings also has a more heavily floral, almost citrusy, aroma and flavor. Although Goldings is primarily thought of as an aroma hop, it can be used for bittering and flavor as well.

Northdown is a versatile, dual-purpose hop with an alpha range of 6.5 to 8.5%. It imparts a clean bitterness and a lightly fruity flavor and aroma.

Northern Brewer is grown in Germany and America, with the latter having a higher myrcene level. It is a mid-alpha hop (8 to 10%) and is most often used as a bittering hop in brown ales.

Nugget is a fairly high-alpha (12 to 14%) hop. It produces a clean, smooth bitterness that is often attributed to its low co-humulone level.

Target is a high-alpha (11 to 16%) English hop that produces very clean bitterness. Some brewers also use it for its fruity, resiny flavor and aroma. However, its high myrcene level makes it less appropriate for English browns.

Willamette is an American cousin of Fuggles and shares many characteristics of that classic English aroma hop. Low in alpha (4 to 5.5%), it has a somewhat earthy aroma and flavor. But it has more myrcene than its English cousin and therefore imparts a more flowery aroma and flavor.

Yeast

English brewers tend to use yeast strains that contribute a distinctive flavor to the finished beer. At times, such strains are used despite the difficulties in managing them, and some unique fermentation systems have evolved to facilitate their use, as we explain in chapter 4.

In North America, where cylindro-conical fermenters populate nearly every brewery, there is a lower tolerance for idiosyncratic yeast strains. Often the strain used for producing brown ale is the same one used for making wheat beer, alt beer, and even cream ale. Not surprisingly, such yeasts provide little in terms of distinctive character; many are simply clean and unobtrusive.

Many of the best brown ales are made at breweries dedicated to ale brewing. In these cases, special yeast strains are selected to deliver a finished product marked by the character of the yeast. Among the brewers we polled, London ale strains were particularly popular. Among homebrewers making British-style browns, the Irish, London, and other full-bodied strains were generally selected.[2]

Beyond these favored yeasts, many strains may be used for the production of brown ales. Craftbrewers today face a dizzying selection. As a result, those who want a truly distinctive product may wish to explore other alternatives. For the homebrewer who enjoys brown ales, the opportunity to experiment with yeast strains is an important part of the search for the perfect pint of brown beer.

Most brewers consider three key factors when choosing a yeast:

1. Attenuation
2. Flocculation
3. Flavor impact

TABLE 8

Yeasts Appropriate for Northern-Style Brown Ales

Dry Yeasts

      Danstar Nottingham
      Munton's Gold
      Yeast Labs Whitbread Ale Yeast

Liquid Yeasts

      Brewers Resource BrewTek
          CL-110 British Microbrewery Yeast
          CL-160 British Draft Ale Yeast
          CL-270
      Head Start #150 English Ale Yeast
      Saccharomyces Supply Company RTP English Ale
      White Labs
          California Ale
          Irish Ale
          British Ale
          Edinburgh
      Wyeast
          #1028 London Ale
          #1098 British Ale
          #1318 London Ale III
          #1335 British Ale II
      Yeast Culture Kit Company
          A17 Pale Ale
          A21
          A59
      Yeast Lab
          A01 Australian Ale
          A04 British Ale

Attenuation refers to the ability of the yeast to metabolize the various sugars available in the wort. A low attenuating yeast can consume only the simplest of sugars, leaving others alone, thereby resulting in a fuller-bodied product. A highly attenuative yeast consumes nearly all fermentable sugars, thereby producing a drier, lighter-bodied beer.

Flocculation is the ability of yeast cells to clump together and form a compact yeast cake during and after fermentation. A highly flocculant yeast quickly clumps and forms a very compact yeast cake, sometimes at the expense of attenuation. A less flocculant yeast stays suspended in the beer longer. This can produce higher attenuation, but it may leave yeast in suspension afterwards, thereby causing haze and filtration problems.

Yeast impacts the flavor of beer in a number of ways. One is the extent to which normal by-products such as fruity esters and diacetyl remain in the finished beer. A second is the emphasis that the yeast may impart to either malt or hop character in the beer. Finally, some yeasts contribute distinctive flavor tones, such as sulfur, mineral, or wood characteristics.

American brewers tend to favor cleaner yeast strains that do not contribute much beyond a pleasant level of fruitiness. In Britain, however, many brewers' yeast

TABLE 9

Yeasts Appropriate for Southern English-Style Brown Ales

Dry Yeasts

    Danstar London
    Yeast Lab Australian Ale

Liquid Yeasts

    Brewers Resource BrewTek
        CL-150 British Real Ale Yeast
    Head Start #152 London Tap
    Saccharomyces Supply Company RTP
        London Special Bitter
        Scotch Ale
    White Labs
        English Ale
        Burton Ale
    Wyeast
        #1084 Irish Ale
        #1318 London Ale III
        #1968 Special London
    Yeast Culture Kit Company
        A15 English Ale
        A20
        A42
        A64
        A65

strains produce distinctive profiles that give a signature flavor to every product. In a broad way, these generalizations can be used in selecting yeast for your brown ales. Go with a clean, straightforward selection—or perhaps one that emphasizes hops—for your American ales. For a British ale, select an authentic strain and embrace the distinctive flavors it contributes.

Because brewing habits and product availability vary rather broadly, you will likely be interested in a selection of appropriate yeast strains rather than a single rigid choice. The following sections provide broad, general descriptions of the yeast characteristics suitable for the various types of brown ales. A list of commercial products that appear to meet those criteria are scattered throughout this chapter.

Northern-Style English Brown Ales

Northern-style English brown ales finish fairly dry, so you want a medium to highly attenuative yeast. A slight amount of diacetyl is acceptable, as are some fruity esters. You also will want a yeast that accentuates malt character. Flocculation can be medium to high, as long as it doesn't interfere with attenuation. The yeasts listed in table 8 meet these criteria.

Southern-Style English Brown Ales

Southern English-style brown ales finish sweeter and with more body, so they require a less attenuative yeast. They can have moderate fruity esters with a slight amount of diacetyl. Possible yeasts are listed in table 9.

TABLE 10

Yeasts Appropriate for American-Style Brown Ales

Dry Yeasts

Danstar Manchester
Munton's Gold
Brewers Resource BrewTek
    CL-10 American Microbrewery Yeast
    CL-20 American Microbrewery Yeast II
    CL-50 California Pub Brewery Ale
Head Start
    #100 No. 1 Ale
    #101 American Ale
Saccharomyces Supply Company RTP
    Acme Ale
    U.S. Ale
White Labs
    California Ale
    German Ale/Kölsch
Wyeast
    #1056 American Ale
    #1272 American Ale II
Yeast Culture Kit Company
    A01 American Ale
Yeast Lab A02 American Ale

American-Style Brown Ales

American-style brown ales tend to favor a yeast strain with medium to high attenuation and that is clean with low levels of esters and little or no diacetyl. A yeast that accentuates the enhanced bitterness and hop character of

TABLE 11

London Water

Mineral	Parts per Million (ppm)
Calcium	50
Magnesium	20
Sodium	100
Carbonate	160
Sulfate	80
Chloride	60

Note: These minerals are ordered according to the net charge of the ion.

these ales will serve you well when the hoppier Texas brown style is made. Table 10 lists possible choices.

Water

In many cases, brewers can approach brown ales with little concern for water chemistry. The dark grains associated with this style nicely compensate for the excess alkalinity that is the most common fault in brewing water. Beyond that, no single mineral component is noted for contributing an essential element to the classic flavor of any of the three brown ale styles.

Still, a few situations merit discussion. We begin with the brewing of the British brown ale styles. Here, only

Yeast Suppliers

Brewers Resource
409 Calle San Pablo, #104
Camarillo, California 93012
800-827-3983

Saccharomyces Supply Company
190 Vanderbilt Avenue
Norwood, Massachusetts 02062

White Labs
9065 Gold Coast Drive
San Diego, California 92126
619-693-3441

Wyeast Laboratories
PO Box 425
Mount Hood, Oregon 97041
541-354-1335

Yeast Culture Kit
1308 West Madison
Ann Arbor, Michigan 48103-4732
313-761-5914

Yeast Lab is distributed by:
G.W. Kent, Inc.
3667 Morgan Road
Ann Arbor, Michigan 48108
800-558-4060

brewers with very soft water need to be overly concerned. This is easily understood when we review the profile for London water, given in table 11.

This profile shows medium-to-high levels of the salient brewing minerals. (Samuel Smith's Yorkshire water is fairly similar.) The purist may proceed to match this water profile in his or her own brewing water with precise water-salt additions. Only those with very soft brewing water, however, should feel required to add mineral supplements.

The Tadcaster water used by Samuel Smith's is drawn from an underground lake resting on a bed of limestone. This hard water source has made Tadcaster one of the largest brewing cities in England and earned it the title of "Burton of the North."

Brewers faced with very soft water may treat it by using calcium chloride alone. By adding enough calcium chloride to contribute 70 ppm of calcium, you also are adding 120 ppm of chloride. Alternatively, gypsum might be used along with a small amount of non-iodized sodium chloride. Adding enough gypsum to contribute 85 ppm of calcium will give you 207 ppm of sulfate; enough salt to give 74 ppm of sodium will give 111 ppm of chloride. These treatments should provide adequate calcium for proper mash chemistry as well as some support for the sweet, rounded flavors of British brown ales. The calcium chloride might be preferred for the sweeter southern style and the gypsum for the slightly crisper northern styles.

With American brown ales, you'll face a different challenge when it comes to water. The maltier American style can be treated much like the British beers. The hoppier Texas style, however, needs a different approach. The substantial bitterness and hop character of this style means that some thought should be given to water chemistry.

With well-bittered beers, the carbonate or alkalinity of brewing water can produce a harsh, unpleasant bitter flavor. Brewers who have high levels of carbonate (more than 160 ppm or so) should make some effort at carbonate reduction.

Homebrewers commonly reduce carbonate through dilution with distilled water or by boiling to precipitate calcium carbonate. In both cases, additional calcium must be added to make up for the effects of treatment. Other salts may be needed as well.

Commercial American brewers often use food-grade acid to compensate for alkaline waters. Used in excess, this acid results in highly acidic and overdry beers that will deviate from the desired brown ale profile. Where possible, ion exchange filters should be used instead to remove carbonate. Alternatively, you can reduce or, in the case of modestly alkaline waters, eliminate the acid treatment altogether.

In Texas brown ales, calcium additions should be made using gypsum. The gypsum contributes not only calcium, but also sulfate, a mineral that helps ensure a crisp bitterness. For the softer American browns, calcium chloride is preferred.

Other Ingredients

Throughout the history of brown ale, herbs, spices, and other flavorings of various types have been added. Some, such as the herbs and spices, played a role now assumed by hops. Others, such as molasses and brown sugar, made brewing more economical or possible when times were hard for brewers. They contributed not only fermentable sugar, but also flavor. Some of these nontraditional ingredients serve only as an alternative source of fermentable sugar. To this day, many British breweries continue to add them to the boil kettle, the fermenter, or the finished beer.

You may choose to include these ingredients in order to sample the beers of a by-gone era or in an effort to accurately reproduce British brewing techniques. In doing so, you may find a new flavor to add as a regular part of your beer inventory.

Sugar

In Britain, some brewers routinely include sugar in the production of their ales. Most sugars have little in the way of flavor components and are fully fermentable. Examples include the following:

Common Name	Constituent Sugar(s)
Table or granulated sugar	Sucrose
Corn sugar	Glucose
Candi sugar	Sucrose
Invert sugar	Glucose and fructose
Corn syrup	Glucose

Sucrose is just common table sugar and is often derived from sugar cane or sugar beets. Newcastle is one brewer that adds sucrose to its boiled wort just before cooling. Glucose (corn sugar or corn syrup) is often used to prime beers before bottle or cask conditioning. Both sucrose and glucose are fully fermentable, so they will add alcohol without adding body. Both can be used for up to 10% of your gravity.

Invert sugar, also called golden syrup in Britain, is a syrup made by heating sucrose in a slightly acidic solution.

The heat partially breaks down the sucrose into its two monosaccharide components, glucose and fructose. Some brewers prefer this syrup to pure sucrose because yeast can more easily digest glucose and fructose.

In general, the use of these sugars should be restricted to no more than 10% of the total fermentable material in the recipe.

Flavored Sugars

When looking at alternative sources of fermentable material, remember that the fermentable sugars give you no direct flavor impact. After all, they are fermented into alcohol and CO_2. (The cidery flavor that comes from adding too much sugar is the result of yeast function and does not come from the sugar itself.) The flavors contributed by some sugar products come from the unfermentable components. These may include unfermentable sugars such as lactose and substances other than sugar that come from the raw material.

To get some real flavor from a sugar or syrup, it must contain some portion of impurities. The impurities from beet sugar are not desirable, so typically the attractive flavors in processed sugar come from sugar cane. Honey may be another source of flavorful impurities. Alternatively, flavor may be created as a result of the heat used to concentrate a sugar solution, for instance when maple syrup is produced.

The following paragraphs list the potentially flavorful sugars that might be used in brewing. Most should be used sparingly until you become familiar with the characters they impart in the beer. All contain fermentable monosaccharides or disaccharides that may disrupt fermentation if used in excess. In addition, some are strongly flavored and can overwhelm the character of the beer rather easily. Again, you should derive no more than 10% of the fermentables from the sugar source, as a start.

Brown sugar: Brown sugar consists of sucrose crystals covered with a coating of molasses.[3] The molasses itself provides the flavor, and the darker it is, the more flavor it has.

Caramel: Caramel is formed when sugar is heated to very high temperatures (400 °F or 204 °C). It can provide both flavor and color. You could experiment with the candy types sold in stores, but who knows what they contain. Alternatively, you can make some of your own from corn syrup or table sugar. See the article by Jeff Frane, "How Sweet It Is—Brewing with Sugar," in the Spring 1994 issue of *Zymurgy*.

Honey: Honey is a naturally highly concentrated form of sugar and includes various impurities that can contribute a distinctive flavor and aroma to a beer. Because of its flavor components, it can be used for almost any portion of the fermentables in a beer (although at a certain point, you are making mead rather than beer!). Avoid boiling in order to retain the honey flavor and aroma compounds.

Lactose: Lactose, also called milk sugar, is not fermentable by brewing yeasts and therefore will remain in the finished beer to provide some residual sweetness. This ingredient is classically used in the production of sweet stouts, which are thereby dubbed "milk stout."

Maple syrup: The sap that runs from maple trees contains only about 2% solids (mostly sugar) and therefore must be concentrated before use. This is done by boiling off water to bring the concentration of solids up to about 66%. As you can imagine, this requires quite a bit of boiling. In the process, a portion of the sugars is caramelized. This caramelizing provides much of the characteristic flavor of maple syrup.

The sugar in maple syrup is mostly sucrose. The majority of commercial products is a blend of one part maple syrup plus four to six parts corn syrup.[4] Since corn syrup is mostly glucose, it offers little in the way of flavor components. Try instead to get some raw or unblended maple syrup that has not been diluted in this manner.

Maple syrup comes in two grades, Grade A and Grade B, with Grade B possessing a stronger flavor and aroma. Many commercial "maple-flavored" syrups, however, are simply corn syrup with maple flavoring added and are not suitable for brewing.

Molasses: Molasses is the residue that results from processing raw sugar cane into sugar. It contains the impurities from the sugar cane that are not wanted in refined sugar. As a result, it also has the most flavor of all of the available sugars and syrups. Molasses comes in three grades: light, medium, and blackstrap. Each successive grade contributes a darker color and a sweeter, fruitier flavor. The lighter grades are more highly fermentable (90%) and have fewer flavor components, while the blackstrap grades are less fermentable (50 to 60%) and have much higher flavor impact.[5] A discernible flavor component can be obtained from one cup of molasses in five gallons of beer. Molasses is most often added during the boil and adds flavor, color, and fermentable sugars.

Palm sugar: Palm sugar is a dark, highly flavored product derived from the sap of palm trees.[6] Its flavors and impact on beer are unknown, but if you check out some Asian specialty stores you might be able to find some with which to experiment.

Raw sugar: Raw sugar is approximately 97% sucrose and 3% ash, invert sugar, organic nonsugars, and water,[7] so it should be highly fermentable and contain little in the way of flavor-producing impurities. If you want to experiment, look for the darkest you can find.

Treacle: Treacle is British molasses. It comes in various colors and grades, as does American molasses.

Turbinado: Turbinado is a form of raw cane sugar sometimes found in America. The comments for raw sugar apply here as well.

Herbs and Spices

Before hops appeared on the English brewing scene, brewers and brewsters used various spices, herbs, and roots to flavor their ales and balance the malty sweetness. Often they would employ a mixture of several spices, thereby providing a bitter contrast to the sweetness of malt, along with distinctive flavors and aromas. The following paragraphs offer a look at some of the herbs and spices used in the past.

Alecost: Alecost, a member of the aster family, has a small yellow flower that contributes a light bitterness and a menthol and sage flavor and aroma.

Alehoof: Alehoof is a small creeping plant that is bitter and aromatic. It is also known as ground ivy, alehove, tunhoof, cat's paw, and gill-over-the-ground or gill-go-by-the-hedge (the latter two are derived from the French *guiller*, which means to ferment). In *The Herbal* or *Generall Historie of Plantes*, written in 1597, J. Gerard writes that alehoof "strengthens and cleanses."

Bay: Bay leaves and berries were used to flavor ales. Bay was said to keep you safe from witchcraft and lightening.

Bayberry: Bayberry leaves and seeds were used to flavor ales. The waxy covering of this shrub's berries was used to make candles.

Birch: The bark of sweet birch was used to make birch beer. The sap was used like maple sap, as a sugar source.

Bog myrtle: The flowers of the bog myrtle shrub were said to induce rapid drunkenness. Also known as sweet gale, it was also used in England to keep fleas out of linens.

Cardamom: Cardamom is a spice that is often mentioned in surviving recipes, but its high cost may have limited its use.

Centaury: Brewers employed the root of the medicinal centaury plant to provide bitterness.

Cinnamon: Cinnamon was used particularly in the spiced wassails of winter.

Clove: Clove was used as a flavoring in ales and blended with aloe to cure flatulence.

Comfrey: The purple and white flower of the comfrey is still popular in herbal teas, but Gerard had a much higher opinion of this wonder herb:

> The slimie substance of the root made in a posset of ale, and given to drink against the paine in the backe, gotten by any violent motion, as wrestling or over much use of women, doth in fower or five daies perfectly cure the same, although the involuntarie flowing of the seed in men may be gotten thereby.

Costmary: The flavoring costmary herb was said to give an ale "good relish and cause it to be somewhat physical in the month of May," according to John Parkinon in 1629.

Dandelion: The dandelion is a common yard weed whose leaves were sometimes put in ale because of their bitterness and diuretic properties.

Elder: Uncooked, the elder is poisonous, but when boiled, its flowers flavored ale.

Eyebright: Eyebright was used to help restore eyesight among the aged when brewed in strong ale.

Hyssop: The oil of hyssop was a cure-all and also used to flavor everything from ales to the liqueur Chartreuse.

Juniper: The berries of the juniper shrub were used to flavor beer and later gin.

Lovage: The stems and fruits of the aromatic lovage plant flavored ales and added bitterness.

Milk thistle: Milk thistle provided a bitterness that is nearly identical to hops.

Mugwort: A roadside herb, mugwort was frequently used by brewers for its spicy flavor.

Nettle: The nettle is a cousin to the hop family and was used to add bitterness. It was also seen as a cure-all for everything from baldness to gout.

Sage: Sage gave an earthy flavor and bitterness.

Tansy: Tansy is now considered a weed and in some states is the focus of state-financed eradication programs. But in medieval England, it was prized for the bitterness it added to ale.

Yarrow: Yarrow leaves were used in medicinal tea and also were said to increase the inebriating qualities of ale.

Much of brown ale comes from its ingredients, especially malt. Those who love the style will catalog the available grains and then brew with each in turn, varying one at a time or changing the entire grist with each recipe. Through such experimentation, one approaches the sublime result—a beer that is at once luxurious and quaffable. In the next chapter, we talk about the brewing processes necessary to craft great brown ale.

CHAPTER 4

Brown Ale Procedures

With the exception of Newcastle Brown Ale, which is a blend of two ales brewed separately and then mixed together, brown ale brewing follows the straightforward brewing techniques long practiced by British brewers. Many North American brewers have already mastered the same techniques, and those who already make good ales will find few surprises in crafting brown ale. Perhaps that accounts for the popularity of the style with homebrewers and craftbrewers across that continent.

Even though most brewers possess the skills needed to brew brown ale, we find that the classic producers engage in some unique techniques. In this chapter, we talk about the brewing practices followed at various breweries that make brown ale. Based on the information we have been able to gather, we comment on the practices in Scottish and Newcastle Breweries' large automated brewery, on the smaller and more traditional English brewing systems such as the one at Samuel Smith's, and on the routine practices of small American breweries. Where appropriate, commentary on how these commercial techniques apply to home-brewing is supplied.

The Hot Side of Brewing

The hot side of brewing includes all of the steps from mash-in to the time that cool wort exits the heat exchanger on its way to the fermenter. In most breweries, only one feature of the hot side is significant, the mash program. While some minor variations in procedure may exist in milling, lautering, and chilling, the management of the mash impacts many other aspects of the process, from the raw materials used and the amount of energy consumption to equipment requirements and finished beer flavor.

Mashing

English brewers have long relied on the simplest mash method, the single infusion mash. But even a simple mash can be carried out in different ways.

In large breweries such as Scottish and Newcastle Breweries, separate vessels are dedicated to mashing and lautering. Cereal cookers are also used, when needed, for the preparation of adjuncts. As at other large breweries, from Pilsen to Plank Road, the brew-house equipment at Scottish and Newcastle Breweries comes in sets, with pairs of mash mixers and lauter tuns kept in continuous operation. The dedication of individual vessels to each part of the process means optimal performance can be achieved while still maintaining efficient use of capital. These larger and more flexible brewing operations may use step infusion mashes to accommodate wheat or higher-protein malts.

In smaller British breweries, as at most small American facilities, a combined mash/lauter vessel is employed. In many cases, these vessels are insulated but unheated—a design that is similar to home mash tuns built from insulated picnic coolers. The unheated vessels hold a mash temperature fairly adequately once it has been achieved. However, on a commercial scale, at least, there are few alternatives for heating a mash that already resides in the vessel.

This common mash/lauter design determines several other aspects of the brewing process. First and foremost, it generally means that the brewer has no option but to use a single mash conversion temperature. Second, it means that the blending of the grist with the hot liquor will determine the temperature of the mash. Finally, it eliminates or hinders the mash-out step, in which the temperature of the mash is raised to 167 °F (75 °C). Brown ale brewers accommodate these limitations through a variety of means.

The single-infusion-mash program suits the use of the well-modified malts, which are nearly always encountered in brown ales. Such malts can be effectively mashed at a single saccharification temperature without the need for a protein rest or other low temperature phase.

Through experience, most brewers learn what temperatures to use when mixing their grist and mash liquor so that the proper rest temperature is achieved. The standard ratio of 1.33 quarts of liquor per pound of grain or 1.1 barrels per 100 pounds is commonly used.

After mixing, slight adjustments to the mash temperature may be accomplished by additions of cold or hot liquor. In some cases, underletting the mash with hot liquor at 190 °F (88 °C) or higher may be used in an effort to raise the temperature significantly.

Hot Scotchie, or the Flying Scotsman

The origins of the following ritual are rather sketchy, but the late Russell Scherer is often credited with introducing it to the craft-brewing scene. Jim learned about hot scotchies from Artie Tafoya on a very cold, snowy day when he was brewing at the Hubcap Brewery in Vail, Colorado.

The process is very simple. Once you have recirculated and clarified your wort, draw off about a pint of first runnings, leaving enough room in the glass for an ounce of good single malt scotch whisky. Add the scotch, mix well, and drink.

The rich malt sugar of the wort combines wonderfully with the whisky—particularly a peatier Islay or lowland scotch—to make a delicious warm drink that gives you a nice energy boost during your brew day.

A hot scotchie at the beginning of the lauter can help to prevent stuck mashes—or at least make them easier to cope with when they occur.

The greatest challenge brewers face with an unheated mash tun is adjusting the mash temperature for the mashout. Underletting may be used at the end of the mash to raise the temperature toward the mash-out level. In addition, the sparge water temperature may be set higher than normal for some or all of the lauter process in an effort to help raise the grain bed temperature. When doing this, brewers must guard against excessive temperatures which will leach tannins from the husks and give the beer an astringent character.

Homebrewers have an added option. They can use an external heat source (also known as a pot on the stove) to perform a decoction or to heat a portion of the first runnings during recirculation as an aid in achieving the mash-out temperature.

For a northern-style brown ale, mash temperatures should be fairly low by American standards, in the range of 150 to 152 °F (66 to 67 °C). The London-style browns require more body and therefore a higher saccharification temperature, in the range of 156 to 158 °F (69 to 70 °C). As in other areas, the American brown ales seem to split this difference, with a medium to medium-full body that suggests a mash temperature of about 154 °F (68 °C). Texas brown ales can be mashed at the same temperature.

Boiling

Brown ales may benefit from longer than normal boils through increased caramelization that adds both color and flavor complexity to the beer. Caramelization occurs when sugar is heated to temperatures above 400 °F (204 °C). This effect generally occurs only at the interface between the heat source and the wort. Flame-heated kettles tend to produce greater caramelization than steam-heated kettles. While Scottish and Newcastle Breweries and most other commercial breweries use steam heat these days, flame-heated kettles are still found. They contribute another unique dimension to the finished beer.

While the English-style browns can be managed with two or even one addition of hops, the American and Texas styles may have more complex hop schedules during the boil. Bittering or kettle hops are generally added near the beginning of the boil. Flavor hops are added at one or more times 10 to 30 minutes before the end of the boil. Aroma hops may be added in the last few minutes of the boil, steeped in the hot wort after the boil, or—if your equipment allows—added to the fermenter during maturation. Cask-conditioned brown ales can be dry hopped in the cask at the rate of one-half ounce of whole aroma hops per firkin.

At the end of the boil, some English brewers, such as Scottish and Newcastle Breweries, add their kettle sugars to the wort. Sugar additions increase the OG of the wort and dry out the finish by increasing overall fermentability as compared to a grain-derived wort. American brewers who use molasses, brown sugar, honey, and other similar ingredients may also add it at the end of the boil, once the heat has been turned off. This procedure allows the hot wort to sanitize the added ingredient. It also eliminates the major loss of aromatic flavor compounds that would occur during boiling. Some of these ingredients may also be added in the fermenter, as detailed later in this chapter.

Separation and Cooling

Most commercial breweries around the world have a whirlpool to separate wort from trub and hop debris. Larger breweries use dedicated whirlpool vessels, while smaller ones often have a kettle that doubles as the whirlpool.

In England, some breweries substitute a settling tank for the whirlpool. Mild ale brewers in the West Midlands often use these shallow rectangular tanks. After the boil, the brewer delivers hot wort to the settling tank. In some cases, hops are added to contribute to the hop aroma of the beer. Then a rest period begins.

According to Stokes's law, the particulate matter suspended in a given liquid settles at a fixed rate. The shallow design of the settling tank allows trub and hops to reach the bottom of the tank more quickly than they would in a deeper kettle or whirlpool vessel. The settling tanks are generally open and uninsulated and present a large surface area for both evaporation and radiation of heat. Thus, the wort cools to a significant degree during this rest. Hind notes that settling-tank rest times may vary from 20 to 90 minutes.[1]

The biggest shortcoming of these open settling tanks is the potential for infection of the wort. To counteract this, time spent in the tank is limited to that required for reasonable wort clarity. The majority of the wort cooling is achieved with a plate and frame (counterflow) heat exchanger. In America, brewers routinely use plate and frame chillers to cool the hot wort drawn from the settled whirlpool.

Fermentation and Conditioning

American brewers see fermentation in fairly monolithic terms. Cylindro-conical fermenters populate nearly every brewery, large and small, and the standard practices for using them are well established. The most significant variable that changes from brewery to brewery or batch to batch relates to the temperature during fermentation.

Our research did not indicate any unusual practices with regard to the fermentation temperatures in producing brown ales either here or in Britain. The actual fermentation temperature employed will depend on the yeast strain that is selected as well as the brewer's own equipment and preferences.

In England, many breweries have operated for 100 years or longer at the same location. Brown ale producer Samuel Smith's, for instance, has been brewing at the same site since 1758. They, like many other brewers with a long brewing heritage, have adopted certain fussy yeast strains because of their flavor characteristics. Generations of brewers have attempted to keep the yeast happy, not only through normal operating parameters such as wort composition and fermentation temperature, but also by using very specific capital equipment.

Two of the most unusual and distinctive fermentation systems found in England are the Yorkshire slate squares and the Burton Union system. Perhaps, surprisingly, both of these rare traditional systems are used to produce distinctive brown ales.

Yorkshire Slate Squares

In Tadcaster, the Samuel Smith's brewery still ferments its beers in Yorkshire slate squares. This unique fermentation system has been used for dozens of years. The 1982 brewing book *Malting and Brewing Science* by J. S. Hough, et al., describes the system:

> Yorkshire Stone Squares were originally vessels made of stone and later, slate. They were therefore of small capacity—46 hl [37 US barrels] was a common capacity. . . . [M]odern materials have largely replaced the traditional ones and modern Yorkshire Squares are of stainless steel. They are characterized by having a lower compartment separated from the upper open portion by a deck. The deck gives entry to the lower vessel by a series of pipes and by a central manhole with

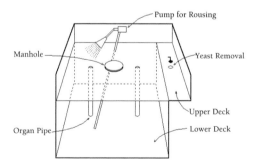

Samuel Smith's Yorkshire slate squares, used for fermentation.

a flange 15 cm (6 in) around the rim. The lower compartment is filled with wort and yeast and the upper to a depth of about 2.5 cm (1 in). Yeast rises through the manhole and remains on the deck while the beer drains back through the pipes. Strongly flocculant yeast strains are used with this system of fermentation and the fermenting wort has to be roused vigorously by a pumping system of circulation. Eventually the yeast on the deck is recovered by stopping the circulation and skimming it away from the deck. The beer is racked off from the lower compartment. The system . . . is claimed to give a characteristic type of beer.[2]

Nearly 40 years earlier, H. Lloyd Hind also wrote about the squares, providing some details about their operation and the final effects on the gravity of the beer:

Normally a number of squares are filled from a wort main, through branch mains, as in other systems. The wort runs from the upper back through the organ pipe, usually occupying a depth of two or three inches in the yeast back, as well as the lower vessel. Pumping usually commences 24–36 hours after collection, the wort mixing with the yeast in the upper vessel and running back through the organ pipe. Pumping for about 10 minutes at a time is repeated every 2–4 hours until the desired attenuation is reached, or about 6 hours before yeast removal is due to commence. Beer or "back drink" is drained from the yeast, which is then run through the side pipe or otherwise removed from the upper back. Yeast still continues to rise through the manhole for 6 to 18 hours, is drained and collected, the lower vessel being kept full of beer.

Though the yeast is always of flocculating character, there are variations in degree. Some strains rise so completely from the wort that attenuation ceases when pumping is terminated. This must consequently be continued until the final gravity is almost reached. Less strongly flocculating races do not cleanse so fully, and attenuation continues through a few degrees after pumping. *The final gravity may be as high as one-half of the original gravity, but attenuation to one-third or one-quarter can be attained if desired."[3]* (emphasis added)

This indicates that full-bodied beers can easily be produced in the Yorkshire square system. Indeed, other brewers may envy the ability to control attenuation to this extent during fermentation.

Yet, this control comes at the cost of continuous wort aeration during fermentation. You may wonder, as we have, what the effect of that aeration alone might have on the flavor of the finished beer. This would be another interesting experiment for those who have the time to undertake it.

Hind points out two other shortcomings of the slate square system. First, low attenuation beers tend to be less biologically stable than more fully attenuated products. Hind notes that brewers using this system often choose high mash saccharification temperatures and short rest times. This is done in an effort to minimize the amount of readily fermentable disaccharides in underattenuated beers so as to discourage microbial infection. Hind offers no data to support the success of this strategy. Based on the exported Samuel Smith's beers, the attenuation achieved by their process seems well within the normal range.

A second shortcoming is, as Hind says, "The frequent return of yeast to the beer leads to flavors that are much appreciated in northern districts of England but may, if pronounced, become a yeast bite. This is largely due to beer that has remained in contact with yeast in the upper back for some time, after fermentation is completed, and can be avoided by wasting this beer instead of mixing it with the bulk."[4]

For brewers whose greatest creative talent comes in the naming of beers that have strayed from their intended course, these potential faults of slate-square brewing should be remembered. The next time you have an oxidized, yeast-bitten beer, you can simply present it as an experiment in Yorkshire-style brewing!

Burton Unions

Marston's brewery in Burton-on-Trent still uses the classic Burton Union fermentation system, even though it has been abandoned by every other Burton-based brewer. Best of all, Marston's has recently been producing specialty ales to complement their regular products. One of these, a Head Brewer's Choice product, is a brown ale fermented exclusively in the unions.

The Burton Union system calls for fermenting beer in a huge collection of wooden barrels, each holding no

Marston's brewery Burton Union fermentation system—a necessity to brew a Head Brewer's Choice product.

more than three to four barrels in volume. Pipes and tubes extend from each barrel to a long, shallow trough that runs above a dozen barrels. One pipe extends directly from the top of the barrel, ending in a hook or "swan neck" that delivers beer and yeast to the trough. A second tube delivers beer back to the barrels from a collection area at the end of each trough. This allows fermenting beer to return to the barrel, thereby maintaining a constant liquid level. Each barrel is fitted with internal attemperation coils for cooling. Yeast collects in the trough; therefore, a non-flocculant strain can be used. By the time fermentation is complete, much of the yeast has been deposited in the trough, where a portion of it is collected for reuse. The beer in the barrels emerges nearly clear and ready for packaging in casks.

The flavor of the beers fermented in this system is much desired by Burton brewers. The costs of construction, maintenance, cleaning, and operation, however, have sent all but Marston's Burton Union systems to the junk yard. Marston's operates three separate Burton rooms. All use wooden barrels with stainless steel troughs. The key difference between the three rooms is the construction of the supporting trunnions. The oldest is made of wood, the second of iron, and the newest—their "modern" union—of stainless steel. All house the distinctive oak barrels of the Burton Union system.

The specialized fermentation systems of Marston's and Samuel Smith's provide some of the romance and poetry to the making of English brown ales. Every beer drinker— and every brewer—longs to enjoy the products that issue from these historic monuments of brewing. These days, beer lovers are lucky enough in most areas of America to find products from both breweries.

Despite continued use of these wonderful systems, many British brewers now rely on cylindro-conical fermenters or other closed, stainless-steel vessels. If you long to brew great brown ale, don't worry. Your existing fermenter, no matter what its shape or construction, should serve the purpose just fine.

Conditioning and Finishing

In Britain, most brown ales are bottled, but some are sold on draft in cask or keg form. Cask products generally receive only a short settling period before packaging. This is conducted at temperatures of 50 °F (10 °C) or so and is intended to bring yeast counts to the level desired (one to three million cells per milliliter) for cask conditioning.

Kegged and bottled beers are filtered before packaging and thus undergo a slightly longer maturation process. Scottish and Newcastle Breweries follow a procedure familiar to most North American brewers: using a low temperature conditioning of only a few days. The reduced temperature at this stage—usually 35 to 40 °F (1 to 5 °C)—helps to speed precipitation of yeast from the beer.

Before dropping the beer temperature to this range, some brewers perform a diacetyl rest, thereby giving the yeast time to reduce excess diacetyl that may have been produced during fermentation. This can be done with a rest at 50 to 70 °F (10 to 21 °C) for 24 to 48 hours. Afterwards, the temperature is dropped to the lower level for yeast removal and clarification.

Some flavor additives—those that do not contain fermentable sugar—may be added directly to the beer at this time. Also, homebrewers and those commercial brewers with suitable equipment can add fermentable materials for a secondary fermentation. Fermentables should first be pasteurized by heating them to 140 to 150 °F (60 to 66 °C) for 5 to 10 minutes and then chilling before adding them to the beer.

Dry hops can also be added during maturation. British brewers generally dry hop in the cask that is sent to the pub. As a result, the dry hop character has a chance to develop over about 10 days to 3 weeks before serving. Brewers with the ability to dry hop in their secondary or serving tanks may be able to achieve similar results.

On a commercial scale, dry hopping is generally done at rates of 1/8 ounce per firkin[5] or 0.7 to 1.4 ounces per barrel. At a homebrew scale, brewers have been known to boost these rates—dry hopping with as much as two ounces of good quality European aroma hops in a five-gallon batch.

The length of your conditioning time will depend on your recipe. Obviously, if you are adding flavorings or hops at the beginning of your conditioning phase, you should allow the beer to mature longer so that these flavors can become fully integrated into the beer. Dry hopping can also occur after filtration, if desired.

Packaging

Brown ale is a style that does quite well either on draft or in bottles. Because it requires no special aging or handling, it is entirely up to you how to package your beer.

The rich malt flavor of a brown ale lends itself to lower carbonation levels than are found in lager styles. So if you are planning to bottle condition your brown ale, you will want to adjust your priming accordingly. Most homebrewing books recommend three-quarters cup of dextrose or one cup of dried malt extract. For brown ales, you can cut that to one-half cup of dextrose or two-thirds cup of dried malt extract. If you are kegging, or counterpressure bottling, you can carbonate English brown ales to about 1.75 volumes of CO_2 and American browns to 1.75 to 2 volumes.

Although brown ale often is not thought of as a classic style for cask conditioning, it works great in this form.

CHAPTER 5

Commercial Examples

As mentioned before in chapter 2, brown ale's popularity is much greater in the United States than in its native England, where only a few examples exist. In the United States, many brewpubs and a dozen microbreweries produce a brown ale. The examples cited in this chapter are all distributed at least regionally in bottles. We tasted each from the bottle to compile the profiles; many we also were able to enjoy on draft.

We start with the English examples available in the United States and then move to the brown ales made in the States, cutting across all of the substyles in the process. Appendix 2 provides a more comprehensive listing of the brown ales produced in North America.

Northern-Style English Brown Ales

Newcastle Brown Ale

Scottish and Newcastle Breweries, Newcastle on Tyne, England.

Color: Light brown, lightly reddish.

Head: Creamy, off-white.

Aroma: A light, toffee-like malt sweetness. No hop aroma detected. Very light diacetyl and slight apple sweet ester.

Malt flavor: Lightly sweet with notes of toffee and a toasted English muffin. Low diacetyl. Very smooth.

Hop bitterness/flavor: Very low bitterness and hop flavor, just enough to balance the malt.

Finish: Dry and crisp.

Body: Low to medium.

Notes: A very smooth, drinkable ale that helped launch brown ale's popularity in England and the United States. Nothing really exciting or remarkable, but a solid brown ale. A great beer with grilled chicken and pasta.

Samuel Smith's Nut Brown Ale

The Old Brewery, Tadcaster, England.

Color: Medium brown.

Head: Thick, tan.

Aroma: Sweet caramel malt aroma, slightly bready. Low to medium diacetyl.

Malt flavor: Biscuity with a sweet toffee flavor. Rich and smooth.

Hop bitterness/flavor: Very subdued hop bitterness and flavor.

Finish: Slightly dry.

Body: Low to medium.

Notes: A smooth and sweet brown ale that is known as strong brown ale in England. Try munching on a bowl of mixed nuts while sipping one of these. A real treat.

London-Style Brown Ales

Cobnut Nut Brown Ale

Tollemache and Cobbold Brewery, Suffolk, England.

Color: Very dark brown, opaque (north of 40 SRM).

Head: Dark tan and creamy.

Aroma: Faint nutty, biscuity notes.

Malt flavor: Appealing nuttiness with a hint of licorice. Some roasted malt.

Hop bitterness/flavor: Modest hop flavor and bitterness.

Finish: Smooth lingering malt.

Body: Full and creamy.

Notes: London-style brown ale with 4.2% ABV. Amazingly drinkable for something so rich.

Harvey's Old Exhibition Brown

Harvey's Breweries, Lewes, England.

Color: Deep ruby brown.

Head: Thick, brown.

Aroma: Rich caramel malt with molasses notes. No hops discernible. Slight hint of plums and sherry. No diacetyl.

Malt flavor: Rich, dark caramel malt flavor. Very sweet but not cloying. The richness of an old ale but only 3.6% ABV. Sherry-like.

Hop bitterness/flavor: Just enough bitterness to keep it from being cloying.

Finish: Wet, lingering.

Body: Full.

Notes: Marketed as an old ale, but low alcohol, dark color, and sweetness place it within the bounds of the southern brown category.

American Brown Ales

Saint Arnold's Brown Ale

Saint Arnold's Brewery, Houston, Texas.

Color: Light brown.

Head: Thick and full, tan in color.

Aroma: Light toffee from caramel malt, a toasted English muffin. No detectable hops. Very faint fruitiness. No diacetyl.

Malt flavor: Light caramel malt sweetness. No dark caramel or chocolate malt flavor.

Hop bitterness/flavor: Very faint.

Finish: Slightly dry and crisp.

Body: Light.

Notes: A very good example of the northern English brown ale from a Texas brewery known for its German-style lagers and bocks.

Acme California Brown Ale

North Coast Brewery, Fort Bragg, California.

Color: Reddish amber to light brown.

Head: Tawny brown, dissipates quickly.

Aroma: A light, toasty malt aroma. Not particularly

sweet. More like lightly toasted bread. Very faint hops. No diacetyl.

Malt flavor: Light, slightly sweet. Smooth and semidry.

Hop bitterness/flavor: Low to medium bitterness and floral hop flavor.

Finish: Dry.

Body: Light.

Notes: This second in North Coast's revival of the old Acme brand is almost a hybrid between a northern English brown and an American brown. The result is very drinkable.

Rock Creek Nutrageous Brown Ale

Rock Creek Brewing Company, Richmond, Virginia.

Color: Mahogany.

Head: Light brown.

Aroma: Very sweet, malty, with notes of brown sugar. Moderate fruity esters. Raisin-like.

Malt flavor: Sweet, toffee-like from caramel malt.

Hop bitterness/flavor: Light bitterness and flavor follow the sweet malt to provide nice balance.

Finish: Long, lingering malt sweetness.

Body: Medium.

Notes: A very sweet brown ale that definitely fits the bill for accompanying a slice of apple pie.

Brooklyn Brown

Brooklyn Brewery, Brooklyn, New York.

Color: Light brown.

Head: Light brown, creamy.

Aroma: Rich, toffee-like caramel malt.

Malt flavor: Very rich, sweet caramel malt flavor with slight chocolate note.

Hop bitterness/flavor: Low to medium hop bitterness and light, spicy hop flavor.

Finish: Smooth, slightly dry.

Body: Medium.

Notes: A rich, easy-drinking northern English brown ale. Serve this with traditional English bangers and mash or a pot pie.

Full Sail Nut Brown Ale

Full Sail Brewing Company, Hood River, Oregon.

Color: Deep brown.

Head: Thick, light brown.

Aroma: Rich caramel malt with a hint of chocolate malt.

Malt flavor: Sweet, caramel malt with lightly roasty chocolate malt undertones.

Hop bitterness/flavor: Light bitterness and low to moderate spicy hop flavor.

Finish: Smooth and lingering.

Body: Medium.

Notes: A great example of the American brown style. Try this one with barbecue.

Pete's Wicked Ale

Pete's Brewing Company, Palo Alto, California.

Color: Deep, mahogany brown.

Head: Thick, light brown.

Aroma: Floral hops with sweet caramel malt.

Malt flavor: Rich, slightly sweet with just a touch of roastiness from chocolate malt.

Hop bitterness/flavor: Medium-high bitterness and a crisp, floral hop flavor.

Finish: Semidry.

Body: Medium.

Notes: The granddaddy of the American brown ale style.

Hex-Nut Brown Ale

Goose Island Brewing Company, Chicago, Illinois.

Color: Pale ruby (17 SRM).

Head: Thick and creamy, deep cream color.

Aroma: Malty with a brown sugar sweetness.

Malt flavor: Nutty, a hint of molasses.

Hop bitterness/flavor: Spicy hop flavor, low bitterness.

Finish: Lingering maltiness with a hint of molasses.

Body: Medium.

Notes: This beer started life as a *dunkelweizen* pitched with the wrong yeast. Now a leading product, it still retains a generous portion of wheat in the recipe.

Red Hook Nut Brown Ale

Red Hood Brewery, Seattle, Washington.

Color: Cherry red highlights, deep amber hue (14 SRM).

Head: Good lace, firm, light cream–colored head.

Aroma: Perfumy, "noble-type" hop character atop a firm toasty malt base.

Malt flavor: Biscuity, bread-crust malt toastiness.

Hop bitterness/flavor: Assertive spicy hop flavor, gentle bitterness.

Finish: Lingering cinnamon-spice hop note.

Body: Medium-light.

Notes: A seasonal blue-line beer with pleasantly assertive hop character. Leans toward the Texas brown style.

Brothers Best Brown Ale

Two Brothers Brewing Company, Warrenville, Illinois.

Color: Dark brown, nearly opaque. Fire-engine red highlights.

Head: Tan and tight.

Aroma: A hint of hops, a hint of chocolate cake.

Malt flavor: Chocolate liqueur with a hint of roastiness.

Hop bitterness/flavor: Clean and balancing bitterness.

Finish: Refreshing balance of bitter and malty.

Body: Medium.

Notes: A big beer from a small brewer—a London brown with American-style hopping.

Oasis Brown Ale

Oasis Brewing Company, Boulder, Colorado.

Color: Wine-grape red.

Head: Creamy and tight, light tan color.

Aroma: Big toasty nose with hints of brown sugar.

Malt flavor: Sweet and toasty on the tongue.

Hop bitterness/flavor: Little hop flavor and subdued bitterness.

Finish: Lingering malt sweetness with a hint of honey.

Body: Fullish.

Notes: A malty antidote to the world's over-hopped ales.

Burley Brown Ale

James Page Brewing Company, Minneapolis, Minnesota.

Color: Red tinted amber.

Head: Tan and tight.

Aroma: Cocoa powder.

Malt flavor: Light chocolate with toasty background.

Hop bitterness/flavor: Modest hop flavor, crisp but unobtrusive bitterness.

Finish: Lingering chocolate notes.

Body: Medium.

Notes: Right down the center of American brown ale.

Five Malt Ale

Devil Mountain Brewing Company, Cincinnati, Ohio.

Color: Mid-amber/red.

Head: Light tan and generous.

Aroma: Caramel sweet malt aroma with a hint of hops.

Malt flavor: Caramel candy with a nutty background.

Hop bitterness/flavor: Touch of spicy hop flavor, moderate bitterness.

Finish: Bitterness tempered by caramel.

Body: Medium-full.

Notes: Full-bodied interpretation with the emphasis firmly on malt.

CHAPTER 6

Enjoying Brown Ale

As much fun as it is to brew beer, the biggest delight always comes in serving it to guests. In this chapter, we consider ways to enjoy brown ale at home and on the road.

Serving Brown Ale

Here are a few tips to ensure that your brown ale is well received, whether you share it with a few fellow homebrewers or serve it to the masses in a popular brewpub.

Use Appropriate Glassware

We are no longer in the Middle Ages, so it isn't necessary to drink out of stoneware mugs. And we are thankfully out of the United States' Dark Ages of beer ignorance, when drinking beer out of any glass instead of straight out

of the bottle was a sign of weakness. The shape of the glass you choose to serve your beer in will affect how the beer's aromatic compounds are either focused or dispersed. And, aroma plays a huge role in flavor perception.

Unlike some beer styles, brown ale does not have a particular shape of glass associated with its serving. But if you consider brown ale's characteristics, it's easy to choose a proper glass.

English browns have a slightly sweet, malty aroma that isn't overpowering, with a small amount of diacetyl and fruity esters. So the best choice is a glass with a fairly wide opening to allow your schnoz plenty of exposure to these somewhat delicate aromas. Also a good choice is a dimpled or paneled mug, as is a straight-sided pint or the English-style pint with the bulge near the rim.

American brown ales have a more assertive aroma, with more hops and a richer malt aroma. A simple pint glass is great for this style.

Keep the Glassware Beer Clean

Nothing ruins the moment when your lips are about to finally meet your beer for that first sweet sip quite like a big, old, fat lipstick smudge on the rim of the glass. Yuck. It's like zeroing in on that first kiss and just as you sneak a last peak before making contact, you see that there's a leftover chunk of spinach between your intended's teeth.

Lip products, soap residue, mildew, finger oils, anything can affect the appearance, head formation and retention, aroma, and flavor of your beer. Carefully clean and rinse your beer glasses. Check your glass for cleanliness before pouring beer into it.

Serve at the Proper Temperature

Like all English ales, brown ales taste better served warmer than you would serve a lager. This means that a serving temperature of 42 to 48 °F (6 to 9 °C) will bring out the malty sweetness and toffee flavors of an English brown and accentuate the hop aroma and complex flavors of an American brown ale.

Serving Brown Ale with Food

In Michael Jackson's *The New World Guide to Beer*, the author quotes Andrew Campbell's *Book of Beer*: "The flavor of beer is not really appropriate to very sweet entremets. . . . there is at least one exception, for brown ale is excellent with apple pie." Jackson goes on to mention other sweets that brown ale goes well with, such as treacle tart and toffee. Nuts, too, are a great accompaniment. These choices are ideal with sweeter London browns and some of their American brothers.

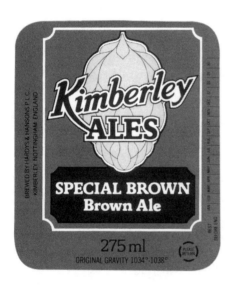

But brown ale's place at the table should not be limited to dessert. We find that brown ales—especially the northern and American types—greatly complement other types of food. The overall complexity of the beer—the fruitiness, maltiness, and just a touch of bitterness in the finish—is the perfect foil for many meat and fish entrees. Try a Samuel Smith's with grilled chicken or even a garlicky pasta dish. The London-type Cobnut would be wonderful with a nice, thick, juicy steak or even a steak-like cut of tuna or salmon. The hoppy Texas-style brown ales are great with grilled and barbecued meats of all kinds. And, try the Red Hook brown with ribs and the Acme California Brown with a mesquite-grilled turkey breast or as the perfect choice with a hearty stew.

In addition, during travels in Japan, we found that brown ales go nicely with sushi and sashimi, while hoppy Texas examples can help to clear the palate when eating tempura or noodles.

And, for the vegetarian brown ale lover, try a Texas brown with grilled eggplant, a sweeter American brown with a cilantro-spiced salad, or a rich brown malty London style with your favorite curry.

Recipes

As an icon of Northeast England, Newcastle Brown, or Newkie, is used in many foods made in that region. For example, one Tyneside bakery makes almost 2,000 breads that include Newkie in the dough.

A key barrier to cooking with beer is the concentrated bitterness that occurs when most beers are reduced through evaporation. Because of this, the less bitter versions of brown—the London and American styles—tend to do well in the preparation of a variety of foods. For example, in *Stephen Beaumont's Brewpub Cookbook*, 10% of the recipes feature brown ale as an ingredient (another 8% call for brown ale as an accompaniment).[1]

No other beer style gets such broad use in the kitchen. Brewpub-tested dishes include everything from Ale-Brewed Chili to Ale-Spiked Smoked Salmon Chowder; Hex-Nut Braised Short Ribs to Peculiar Pork Tenderloin; and Rogue Ale Fish and Chips to Red Tail Pizza. Many brewers are also adventurous cooks who whip up their own recipes for the dinner table. To get you started, we've included a few recipes here.

Brown Town Bread

1-1/2 c. whole wheat flour
1-1/2 c. bread flour
4 tsp. baking powder
2 tsp. salt
1 tbl. honey
12 oz. American or London brown ale (1 bottle or can)

Preheat oven to 350 °F, and grease a 9 x 5-inch loaf pan. Combine all ingredients in a large bowl, stir until well-mixed, and spread in the loaf pan. Bake at 350 °F for 45 minutes or until browned. Remove from the pan. Cool on a rack before slicing.

Cheesehead Brown Ale Bread

    1 package bread yeast
    1/2 c. very warm water
    1 tbl. sugar
    2 c. whole wheat flour
    1 c. plus 3 tbl. white flour
    1 tsp. salt
    1 tbl. butter
    10 oz. brown ale, at room temperature
    4 oz. cheddar cheese, grated
    1 tbl. cooking oil

Proof the yeast by mixing sugar into very warm water and then by adding yeast. Set aside. Add 3 cups flour plus the salt to a large mixing bowl. Melt the butter and add it to the mixing bowl. When the yeast has dissolved in the water, add it and the beer to the mixing bowl and thoroughly blend. This should yield a very sticky mass of dough. By sprinkling additional flour 1 or 2 tablespoons at a time, you want to begin kneading the dough to its final consistency. At the final desired consistency, the dough should be fairly firm

and will separate from your hands when you put it down.

Next, form the dough into a ball and coat with oil. Place it back in the mixing bowl and put in a warm location to rise for 30 to 60 minutes. When the dough has doubled in size, knead in the grated cheese. Divide the dough into two equal parts and form each to fit the bottom of your greased 9 x 4 x 4-inch bread pans. Place the dough in the pans and place in a warm place to let the dough rise.

Preheat the oven to 350 °F.

When the dough has doubled in size again, put it in the oven to bake for 40 to 50 minutes. When finished, remove from the pan and cool on a bread rack.

This recipe produces a delicious, light brown loaf of bread with a mild cheese flavor.

Rosemary Brown Ale Bread

Using the previous recipe, Cheesehead Brown Ale Bread, substitute the cheddar cheese with 1/2 teaspoon of crushed, dried rosemary. The rosemary lends a subtle, but noticeable, character to a full-bodied wheat bread.

Gruit Soup

1 medium onion, chopped
2 tbl. margarine or butter
12 oz. malty brown ale
1/2 c. carrot, finely chopped
1/2 c. celery, finely chopped
2 c. chicken broth
1 tsp. salt
1 tsp. ground cumin
1/4 tsp. ground nutmeg
1 clove
Dash of ground pepper
1 c. dairy sour cream
4 oz. cheddar cheese, grated for garnish

In a 2-quart saucepan, cook the chopped onion in margarine or butter. Add brown ale, carrot, and celery. Heat to boiling, then reduce, cover, and simmer for 10 minutes. Next add everything except the sour cream and the cheese. Stir and heat to a boil, then reduce the head, cover, and simmer for 30 minutes. At the end of the 30 minutes, remove the pan from the stove, add the sour cream, and stir. Ladle into bowls and sprinkle each serving with cheese.

The unusual spices in this soup remind us of the spices once used in gruit to balance the sweetness of beer. This combination of ingredients makes a hearty soup that is one of the best beer recipes ever tried—the perfect restorative after a hard day of brewing!

Bachelor Stew

Here's a one-pot recipe perfected by Joe Coleman of Austin, Texas. He says it's great on cold, blustery days, and excellent accompanied by corn bread, warm muffins, or Brown Town Bread.

1 medium to large onion, chopped

2 tbl. olive oil

1–2 cloves garlic, diced—optional

1 lb. stew meat

Your choice of fresh vegetables, including any or all of the following:

2 brown potatoes

6 stalks celery

4 large carrots

3 tomatoes

1 green bell pepper, seeded

1 red bell pepper, seeded

1 yam or sweet potato

1 or 2 ears of corn-on-the-cob

24 oz. brown ale (2 bottles or cans)

Salt and pepper to taste

Other seasonings of your choice to taste

1 tbl. corn starch or flour

In a Dutch oven or large pot, sauté the onions in the olive oil. If you like, add the garlic when the onions are transparent but do not brown the garlic. Add the stew meat, stirring while it browns.

Chop the vegetables into large chunks. Potatoes can be either peeled or unpeeled. Add salt and pepper to taste, plus other seasonings of your choice. Add the beer. Bring all to a simmer, reduce heat, and cover. Cook for several hours or until the meat is tender and can be cut or broken up with a fork.

Thicken by removing some of the liquid and mixing it with flour or corn starch until

all lumps are dissolved. Slowly add this mixture to the stew, mixing thoroughly. Cook for a few more minutes, and then serve.

Newcastle Brown Mustard Beef 'n' Bacon

1/2 oz. (15 g) flour
Salt and pepper to taste
1-1/2 lb. (700 g) braising steak, cut into thin strips
2 oz. (50 g) bacon, diced
2 oz. (50 g) butter
1 tbl. (15 ml) oil
3 large onions, thinly sliced
1/2 pt. (300 ml) Newcastle Brown Ale
1/2 pt. (300 ml) beef stock
5 tsp. French mustard
1 bouquet garni
8 slices French bread
Chopped parsley

Combine flour, salt, and pepper in a paper or plastic bag. Toss the steak in the seasoned flour. Brown the bacon in the butter and oil in a pan, and then transfer to a casserole dish. Sauté the onions in the pan. Add the beef, and brown on both sides. Place all in the casserole dish.

Sprinkle the remaining seasoned flour in the pan, and slowly stir in the Newcastle Brown Ale, beef stock, and 1 teaspoon of the French mustard. Bring to a boil and simmer for a few minutes, stirring continuously until it reaches the consistency of gravy.

Transfer all to the casserole dish, scraping juices from the pan, and add the remaining seasoning and the bouquet garni. Cover the casserole dish. Cook in oven at 350 °F (180 °C, gas 4) for 1-1/2 hours or until the beef is tender.

Remove from the oven, remove the bouquet garni, and adjust seasoning to taste.

Spread the French bread slices with remaining French mustard, and arrange the slices on the top of the beef in the casserole dish. Cook uncovered in oven for 15 to 20 minutes. Remove from the oven and sprinkle with chopped parsley.

Serve with boiled potatoes and carrots.

Preparation time: 30 minutes

Cooking time: 2 hours

Serves: 6

Beef a la Newcastle Brown

1 tbl. (15 ml) oil

1 lb. (454 g) lean cubed beef

2 cloves garlic
1/2 oz. (15 g) flour
1/2 pt. (300 ml) Newcastle Brown Ale
8 oz. (250 g) onions
8 oz. (250 g) bacon

Heat the oil and brown the beef for 8 to 10 minutes. Add the garlic and flour, mix well, and cook for 1 minute. Stir in the Newcastle Brown Ale and bring to a boil. Cover and simmer for 1-1/2 hours. Add the onions and bacon and cook further for 1 hour.

Preparation time: 20 minutes
Cooking time: 2-1/2 hours
Serves: 6

CHAPTER 7

Recipes for Brown Ales

No book on brewing would be complete without some inviting recipes for you to try. In this section, we present 10 brews that range from pre-industrial smoky brown ale to late twentieth-century flavored beer treats. Each recipe is based on our brewing experiences, so the malt and hop quantities are what worked best for us at the time we brewed the ales. By following these recipes, you should be able to produce enjoyable results in every case.

For advanced homebrewers and commercial brewers, note that nearly all recipes were tested at the five-gallon scale. The amounts given for one barrel are just the five-gallon values multiplied by six. This assumes a 3%

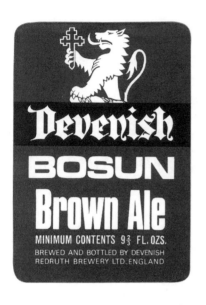

improvement in brew-house efficiency and hop utilization in larger-scale brews. Regardless of batch size, more advanced brewers may want to calculate the specific amounts of grain and hops needed based on the efficiency and utilization of their own brewing systems. To facilitate this, we provide the OG and IBU targets for each beer.

The recipes begin with a historical entry—a smoky brown ale. This one relies on hardwood-smoked malt from the Weyermann maltings in Germany to achieve its authentic wood-smoked flavor.

Of course, no collection of brown ale recipes would be complete without a Newcastle Brown Ale clone. The one we provide is based on Graham Wheeler and Roger Protz's recipe in their book, *Brew Classic European Beers at Home*. Other experimental formulations used more sugar and corn grits in an effort to match the Newcastle Brown Ale formulation as well as its flavor. But the version included here won out in the taste department.

A second English in the northern Newcastle style is Northbound Brown. Jim developed this beer while head brewer at Dimmer's Brewpub in Fort Collins, Colorado. The pub's best-selling beer was a deep brown Scottish ale; the entry included here is a lighter brown ale for summer.

On the London brown front, we couldn't bring ourselves to include the kinds of sugars so often used in this type of beer. For those who want to experiment with sugar, our second example of this style, Treacle Treat, uses molasses for flavor, color, and fermentables.

Like most craftbrewers, we are a couple of hop heads, so we had to include two examples of the Texas-style American brown ale. Both the Texas Tornado and Tumbleweed Brown tip their hats to the Foam Rangers homebrew club in Houston, Texas, whose annual Dixie Cup competition is thought to be the birthplace of the style.

The maltier American-style brown ale has a large following among those who aren't beer fanatics. Neither of us, however, had a good example of the style in our own portfolio, so we made one up! The Lodge calls on a variety of grains—Munich, caramel, wheat, chocolate, and roasted barley—to produce a deeply colored, full-flavored brown ale. It will please most craft-beer drinkers, whether they come from the pub down the road or the peak of the nearest mountain.

Finally, we come to the wacky end of things. Brewers once used spices out of necessity and sugars for economy. These days, neither necessity nor economy motivates the novel flavors found in some brown ales. Instead, we brew with odd things just to see what they will taste like. To provide some reasonable range of possibilities, we include three recipes for your brewing pleasure. The first uses maple syrup, the second hazelnut extract, and the last a smattering of spices that would do any wassail proud.

Let's see . . . that covers lighter and darker, bitter and malty, smoked, mapled, hazelnutted, and spiced. If you or anyone in your household or establishment can't find *something* you're willing to die for here, then we guess you just don't like brown ale!

Pre-Eighteenth-Century Brown Ale

Alewife Brown

Alewife Brown is a highly quaffable, smoky brown brew that goes back to the earliest days of brown ale. The smoke flavor in this beer is nicely balanced by the roasty malt character and the subtle, but evident, hop character. A nice beer on cask.

Malt	Extract or Grain 5 Gal.	All-Grain 5 Gal.	All-Grain 1 Bbl.
Pale Malt Extract Syrup	4.00 lb.	—	—
Weyermann Rauch Malt	2.50 lb.	2.50 lb.	15.00 lb.
Caramel Malt (60 °L)	12.00 oz.	12.00 oz.	4.50 lb.
Black Patent Malt	8.00 oz.	6.00 oz.	2.25 lb.
Munich or Mild Malt	—	6.00 lb.	36.00 lb.

Hops	Extract or Grain 5 Gal.	All-Grain 5 Gal.	All-Grain 1 Bbl.
Willamette (75 minutes)	1.50 oz.	1.50 oz.	9.00 oz.
Liberty (10 minutes)	0.25 oz.	0.25 oz.	1.50 oz.

Yeast
Wyeast #1084 Irish Ale

Brewing Specifics
Partial mash:	Steep grains in 2.5 gallons of 160 °F (71 °C) water for 30 minutes.
Mash:	Infusion mash at 150 °F (66 °C) for 90 minutes.
Boil:	75 to 90 minutes
OG:	1.040
FG:	1.008
Target IBU:	25
Ferment temp.:	68 °F (20 °C)

Northern-Style English Brown Ales

Colonel Porter's Pride and Joy

In the tradition of Newcastle Brown Ale, this beer is made by blending two separate beers. It was inspired by Graham Wheeler and Roger Protz's recipe in *Brew Classic European Beers at Home,* although the proportions of sucrose and pale malt have been changed based on our experience.

First, brew beer 1 and allow it to condition for three weeks. Then brew beer 2 and allow it to condition one week after fermentation. Next blend 1 part of beer 1 to 2 parts beer 2. You'll have 2.5 gallons of the strong beer left to enjoy separately.

Beer 1

Malt	Extract or Grain 5 Gal.	All-Grain 5 Gal.	All-Grain 1 Bbl.
Pale Malt Extract	8.00 lb.	—	—
Caramel Malt (40 °L)	2.00 lb.	2.00 lb.	12.00 lb.
Chocolate Malt	2.00 oz.	2.00 oz.	12.00 oz.
English Pale Malt	—	10.00 lb.	60.00 lb.

Sugar	Extract or Grain 5 Gal.	All-Grain 5 Gal.	All-Grain 1 Bbl.
Sucrose	1.00 lb.	1.00 lb.	6.00 lb.

Hops	Extract or Grain 5 Gal.	All-Grain 5 Gal.	All-Grain 1 Bbl.
Target (60 minutes)	0.75 oz.	0.75 oz.	4.50 oz.
Northern Brewer (30 minutes)	1.00 oz.	1.00 oz.	6.00 oz.

Yeast

Wyeast #1318 London Ale III

Brewing Specifics

Partial mash:	Steep grains in 1 gallon per pound of 160 °F (71 °C) water for 30 minutes.
Mash:	Infusion mash at 153 °F (67 °C) for 90 minutes.
Boil:	90 minutes; add sucrose at end of the boil
OG:	1.070
FG:	1.010
Target IBU:	44
Ferment temp.:	68 °F (20 °C)

Beer 2

Malt	Extract or Grain 5 Gal.	All-Grain 5 Gal.	All-Grain 1 Bbl.
Pale Malt Extract	3.50 lb.	—	—
Caramel Malt (40 °L)	0.75 lb.	0.75 lb.	4.50 lb.
Chocolate Malt	0.75 oz.	0.75 oz.	4.50 oz.
English Pale Ale Malt	—	4.50 lb.	27.00 lb.

Sugar	Extract or Grain 5 Gal.	All-Grain 5 Gal.	All-Grain 1 Bbl.
Sucrose	0.50 lb.	0.50 lb.	3.00 lb.

Hops	Extract or Grain 5 Gal.	All-Grain 5 Gal.	All-Grain 1 Bbl.
Target (60 minutes)	0.50 oz.	0.50 oz.	3.00 oz.
Northern Brewer (30 minutes)	0.75 oz.	0.75 oz.	4.50 oz.

Yeast

Wyeast #1318 London Ale III

Brewing Specifics

Partial mash:	Steep grains in 1 gallon per pound of 160 °F (71 °C) water for 30 minutes.
Mash:	Infusion mash at 153 °F (67 °C) for 90 minutes.
Boil:	90 minutes; add sucrose at end of boil
OG:	1.030
FG:	1.008
Target IBU:	26
Ferment temp.:	68 °F (20 °C)

Finished Blend (1 part Beer 1; 2 parts Beer 2)

OG:	1.043
FG:	1.009
Target IBU:	32

Northbound Brown

This beer was originally brewed to celebrate the opening of a new bridge connecting Dimmer's brewpub with downtown Fort Collins, Colorado. For the opening, the brewpub planned a bike rally across the bridge; the "Northbound" brown commemorated the event. The beer, with its lightly sweet flavor, was a hit. The bike rally wasn't.

Malt	Extract or Grain 5 Gal.	All-Grain 5 Gal.	All-Grain 1 Bbl.
Pale Malt Extract	5.30 lb.	—	—
Caramel Malt (40 °L)	1.00 lb.	1.00 lb.	6.00 lb.
Biscuit Malt	4.00 oz.	4.00 oz.	1.50 lb.
English Pale Ale Malt	—	7.00 lb.	40.00 lb.

Hops	Extract or Grain 5 Gal.	All-Grain 5 Gal.	All-Grain 1 Bbl.
Challenger (60 minutes)	1.00 oz.	1.00 oz.	6.00 oz.
Fuggles (30 minutes)	0.50 oz.	0.50 oz.	3.00 oz.

Yeast

Wyeast #1098 British Ale

Brewing Specifics

Partial mash:	Steep grains in 1.5 gallons of 160 °F (71 °C) water for 30 minutes.
Mash:	Infusion mash at 152 °F (67 °C) for 90 minutes.
Boil:	90 minutes
OG:	1.050
FG:	1.012
Target IBU:	33
Ferment temp.:	68 °F (20 °C)

Southern English Brown Ales

Big Ben Brown

True to the London-style brown ales, this beer is sweet and dark but still light enough to be very drinkable. Great with dessert and for cooking, too.

Malt	Extract or Grain 5 Gal.	All-Grain 5 Gal.	All-Grain 1 Bbl.
Pale Malt Extract	3.75 lb.	—	—
CaraPils	4.00 oz.	4.00 oz.	1.50 lb.
Caramel Malt (120 °L)	8.00 oz.	8.00 oz.	3.00 lb.
Chocolate Malt	2.00 oz.	2.00 oz.	12.00 oz.
English Pale Ale Malt	—	5.00 lb.	30.00 lb.

Hops	Extract or Grain 5 Gal.	All-Grain 5 Gal.	All-Grain 1 Bbl.
East Kent Goldings (60 minutes)	0.50 oz.	0.50 oz.	3.00 oz.
East Kent Goldings (30 minutes)	0.50 oz.	0.50 oz.	3.00 oz.

Yeast

Brewers Resource BrewTek CL-150 British Real Ale Yeast

Brewing Specifics

Extract/grains:	Steep grains in 1 gallon of 160 °F (71 °C) water for 30 minutes.
Mash:	Infusion mash at 158 °F (70 °C) for 90 minutes.
Boil:	After the first half-gallon of wort is in the kettle, turn on the heat source and slowly bring contents to a boil, stirring constantly. Boil for 1 minute to caramelize sugars but be careful not to scorch. Turn off heat and continue adding wort until you reach full volume. Boil full volume for 90 minutes.
OG:	1.038
FG:	1.016
Target IBU:	18
Ferment temp.:	68 °F (20 °C)

Treacle Treat

This experimental ale includes both black treacle and Belgian Special "B" malt, but it delivers the desired results: the sweet, almost raisin-like aroma and flavor of a London brown. If your local supplier doesn't carry brown malt, you can make your own (see the sidebar in chapter 3) or substitute 75% 80 °L caramel malt and 25% chocolate malt.

Malt	Extract or Grain 5 Gal.	All-Grain 5 Gal.	All-Grain 1 Bbl.
Pale Malt Extract	3.50 lb.	—	—
CaraPils	4.00 oz.	4.00 oz.	1.50 lb.
Special "B" Malt	8.00 oz	8.00 oz.	3.00 lb.
Beeston Brown Malt	8.00 oz.	8.00 oz.	3.00 lb.
Chocolate Malt	2.00 oz.	2.00 oz.	2.00 oz.
English Pale Ale Malt	—	4.50 lb.	27.00 lb.

Sugar	Extract or Grain 5 Gal.	All-Grain 5 Gal.	All-Grain 1 Bbl.
Black Treacle (Molasses)	8.00 oz.	8.00 oz.	3.00 lb.

Hops	Extract or Grain 5 Gal.	All-Grain 5 Gal.	All-Grain 1 Bbl.
Target (60 minutes)	0.50 oz.	0.50 oz.	3.00 oz.
Fuggles (30 minutes)	0.50 oz.	0.50 oz.	3.00 oz.

Yeast

Wyeast #1318 London Ale III

Brewing Specifics

Extract/grain:	Steep grains in 1.5 gallons of 160 °F (71 °C) water for 30 minutes.
Mash:	Infusion mash at 158 °F (70 °C) for 90 minutes.
Boil:	90 minutes; add black treacle at end of boil
OG:	1.040
FG:	1.016
Target IBU:	24
Ferment temp.:	68 °F (20 °C)

American Brown Ales

Texas Tornado

Texas, hops; hops, Texas. Any questions?

Malt	Extract or Grain 5 Gal.	All-Grain 5 Gal.	All-Grain 1 Bbl.
Pale Malt Extract	7.00 lb.	—	—
CaraPils	4.00 oz.	4.00 oz.	1.50 lb.
Special Roast	4.00 oz.	4.00 oz.	1.50 lb.
Caramel Malt (80 °L)	8.00 oz.	8.00 oz.	3.00 lb.
Chocolate Malt	1.00 oz.	1.00 oz.	6.00 oz.
American Two-Row Pale Malt	—	9.00 lb.	54.00 lb.

Hops	Extract or Grain 5 Gal.	All-Grain 5 Gal.	All-Grain 1 Bbl.
Galena (75 minutes)	1.00 oz.	1.00 oz.	6.00 oz.
Galena (45 minutes)	0.50 oz.	0.50 oz.	3.00 oz.
Willamette (15 minutes)	0.50 oz.	1.00 oz.	6.00 oz.
Cascade (0 minutes)	1.00 oz.	1.00 oz.	6.00 oz.
Cascade (dry hop)	1.00 oz.	1.00 oz.	6.00 oz.

Yeast
Wyeast 1056, White Labs A02

Brewing Specifics

Extract/grain:	Steep grain in 1 gallon of 160 °F (71 °C) water for 30 minutes.
Mash:	Infusion mash at 154 °F (68 °C) for 90 minutes.
Boil:	90 minutes
OG:	1.056
FG:	1.012
Target IBU:	60
Ferment temp.:	68 °F (20 °C)

Dry hop technique: Steam whole leaf hops in bamboo rice steamer for 15
minutes before adding, after racking, to secondary.

Tumbleweed Brown

Hops take the lead in another Texas-style brown ale.

Malt	Extract or Grain 5 Gal.	All-Grain 5 Gal.	All-Grain 1 Bbl.
Pale Malt Extract Syrup	4.00 lb.	—	—
Caramel Malt (60–80 °L)	1.25 lb.	1.25 lb.	7.50 lb.
Chocolate Malt	8.00 oz.	6.00 oz.	2.25 lb.
Victory, Aromatic, Biscuit, or Special Roast	1.00 lb.	1.00 lb.	6.00 lb.
Pale Ale or Mild Ale Malt	—	9.75 lb.	59.00 lb.

Hops	Extract or Grain 5 Gal.	All-Grain 5 Gal.	All-Grain 1 Bbl.
Chinook (90 minutes)	0.50 oz.	0.50 oz.	3.00 oz.
Cascade (90 minutes)	0.50 oz.	0.50 oz.	3.00 oz.
Cascade (15 minutes)	1.00 oz.	1.00 oz.	6.00 oz.
Cascade (steep 10 minutes at end of boil)	1.00 oz.	1.00 oz.	6.00 oz.

Yeast
Wyeast #1056 American Ale Yeast

Brewing Specifics
Partial mash:	Steep grains in 1.5 gallons of 160 °F (71 °C) water for 30 minutes.
Mash:	Infusion mash at 152 °F (67 °C) for 90 minutes.
Boil:	90 minutes
OG:	1.052
FG:	1.012
Target IBU:	50
Ferment temp.:	68 °F (20 °C)

Be sure to reduce the carbonate content of your brewing water if it exceeds 100 ppm. Add gypsum for any needed calcium supplement.

The Lodge Brown Ale

Like the brown brewed at most brewpubs, this one is malt balanced for those who are in the mood for hops. It offers a dark brown color, a complex malt profile, and a malty finish to make a quaffable restorative to enjoy after a hard day skating, skiing, or just watching the grass grow.

Malt	Extract or Grain 5 Gal.	All-Grain 5 Gal.	All-Grain 1 Bbl.
Pale Malt Extract Syrup	4.00 lb.	—	—
Caramel Malt (60–80 °L)	1.00 lb.	1.00 lb.	6.00 lb.
Munich Malt	1.00 lb.	1.00 lb.	6.00 lb.
Wheat Malt	0.50 lb.	0.50 lb.	3.00 lb.
Chocolate Malt	3.00 oz.	3.00 oz.	1.00 lb.
Roasted Barley	1.50 oz.	1.50 oz.	9.00 oz.
Pale Ale or Mild Ale Malt	—	7.50 lb.	45.00 lb.

Hops	Extract or Grain 5 Gal.	All-Grain 5 Gal.	All-Grain 1 Bbl.
Perle (75 minutes)	0.50 oz.	0.50 oz.	3.00 oz.
Mt. Hood (10 minutes)	0.50 oz.	0.50 oz.	3.00 oz.

Yeast

Wyeast #1084 Irish Ale Yeast

Brewing Specifics

Partial mash:	Steep grains in 1.5 gallons of 160 °F (71 °C) water for 30 minutes.
Mash:	Infusion mash at 154 °F (68 °C) for 60 minutes.
Boil:	90 minutes
OG:	1.048
FG:	1.013
Target IBU:	22
Ferment temp.:	68 °F (20 °C)

Flavored American Brown Ales

Log Cabin Brown

Maple browns have become increasingly popular, particularly in Jim's house. This is a version of a recipe he planned to brew at Dimmer's until the nearby Tommyknocker Brewery came out with a maple brown just a few weeks before Dimmer's opened. Sometimes timing is everything in the beer business. These days, there are enough maple browns out there that he's planning to dust off this recipe and brew it at the Wolf Tongue in Nederland, Colorado.

Malt	Extract or Grain 5 Gal.	All-Grain 5 Gal.	All-Grain 1 Bbl.
Pale Malt Extract	5.50 lb.	—	—
Special Roast	4.00 oz.	4.00 oz.	1.50 lb.
Caramel Malt (40 °L)	8.00 oz.	8.00 oz.	3.00 lb.
Caramel Malt (80 °L)	4.00 oz.	4.00 oz.	1.50 lb.
American Pale Two-Row	—	7.00 lb.	42.00 lb.

Sugars	Extract or Grain 5 Gal.	All-Grain 5 Gal.	All-Grain 1 Bbl.
Pure Maple Syrup	8.00 oz.	8.00 oz.	3.00 lb.

Malt	Extract or Grain 5 Gal.	All-Grain 5 Gal.	All-Grain 1 Bbl.
Centennial (60 minutes)	1.00 oz.	1.00 oz.	6.00 oz.
Willamette (30 minutes)	0.50 oz.	0.50 oz.	3.00 oz.

Yeast

Wyeast 1056

Brewing Specifics

Extract/grain:	Steep grain in 1 gallon of 160 °F (71 °C) water for 30 minutes.
Mash:	Infusion mash at 152 °F (67 °C) for 90 minutes.
Boil:	90 minutes
OG:	1.052
FG:	1.016
Target IBU:	40
Ferment temp.:	68 °F (20 °C)
Maple syrup addition:	After racking into secondary

Old Ogden Spiced Ale

This brew was whipped together as a grain-extract brew and fermented in a bar where the Chicago Beer Society was preparing to hold a homebrew competition many years ago. Given the slap-dash preparation, it wasn't expected to be worth much when finished. Despite this, it wound up being a wonderful balance of malt and spice. A great starting point for a Christmas beer or the next Renaissance Fair.

Malt	Extract or Grain 5 Gal.	All-Grain 5 Gal.	All-Grain 1 Bbl.
Pale Malt Extract Syrup	8.00 lb.	—	—
Caramel Malt (80 °L)	3.00 lb.	3.00 lb.	18.00 lb.
Pale Ale Malt	1.00 lb.	13.00 lb.	78.00 lb.

Hops and Spices	Extract or Grain 5 Gal.	All-Grain 5 Gal.	All-Grain 1 Bbl.
East Kent Goldings (60 minutes)	2.00 oz.	2.00 oz.	12.00 oz.
Cascade (5 minutes)	1.00 oz.	1.00 oz.	6.00 oz.
Allspice (5 minutes)	1/2 tsp.	1/2 tsp.	1 tbs.
Ground Clove (5 minutes)	1/4 tsp.	1/4 tsp.	1-1/2 tsp.
Cinnamon (5 minutes)	1 tsp.	1 tsp.	2 tbs.
Cardamom (5 minutes)	2 seeds, crushed	2 seeds, crushed	18 seeds, crushed
Grated Lemon Peel (5 minutes)	1 tbs.	1 tbs.	6 tbs.
Cascade (steeped at end of boil)	1.00 oz.	1.00 oz.	6.00 oz.
Grated Lemon Peel (steeped)	1 tbs.	1 tbs.	6 tbs.

Yeast

Wyeast #1056 American Ale

Brewing Specifics

Extract/grain:	Steep grains in 2 gallons of 160 °F (71 °C) water for 30 minutes.
Mash:	Infusion mash at 154 °F (68 °C) for 60 minutes.
Boil:	90 minutes
OG:	1.074
FG:	1.028
Target IBU:	50
Ferment temp.:	68 °F (20 °C)

Age for 1 to 3 months before consumption.

How to Calculate International Bitterness Units

IBUs are expressed as the parts per million of iso-alpha-acid that occur in beer. In metric units, this conveniently works out to be the number of milligrams per liter.

You can easily determine the amount of alpha acid added to each beer by multiplying the weight of hops added by the alpha-acid percentage. To find the amount that winds up in the finished beer, you multiply the amount of alpha acid by a utilization rate. Thus, the basic equation for determining IBUs is simple.

What is more difficult is determining the proper utilization factor. Simply stated, utilization tells what percentage of the alpha acids added appears as iso-alpha-acids in the finished beer. The real trick to the accurate estimation of the IBUs from any recipe comes from using the proper utilization factor in your calculations. A basic set of utilization assumptions is given in table A on page 173. With some experience, you will be able to adjust these values to more closely meet your actual experience.

Following is the basic equation for estimating the IBUs obtained from a recipe:

$$\text{IBU} = \frac{W_{oz} \times U\% \times A\% \times 7{,}489}{V_{gal} \times C_{gravity}} \qquad (\text{IBU } \#1)$$

where W_{oz} = weight of hops in ounces,

$U\%$ = percent utilization, again as a decimal (as a starting point, you can determine the utilization for each hop addition on the basis of the number of minutes the hops are boiled, as shown in table A),

$A\%$ = alpha-acid level of hop, as a decimal (for example, 7% = 0.07),

V_{gal} = volume of final wort in gallons, and

$C_{gravity}$ = correction for worts that have a gravity above 1.050 *during boiling.*

Since IBUs are equal to milligrams of iso-alpha-acid per liter of beer, the equation is designed to convert the available information into those terms. The top part of the equation (the numerator) quantifies iso-alpha-acid by multiplying the weight of the hops (in ounces) (W_{oz}) by the utilization factor (U%) by the alpha-acid con-

centration (A%). The final element in the numerator is a correction factor (7,489) that converts the units of the equation into milligrams per liter. The bottom part of the equation (denominator) deals with volume by multiplying the finished volume in gallons (V_{gal}) times a correction factor that relates to wort gravity ($C_{gravity}$).

The volume of final wort in gallons (V_{gal}) should be equal to the greater of (1) the final volume in your boil kettle or (2) the total volume of wort in your fermenter before the yeast is added. (See the examples that follow.)

Correcting for worts that have a OG above 1.050 *during boiling* ($C_{gravity}$) applies to every beer with a target OG greater than 1.050. It also includes most situations in which you boil a concentrated wort that is then diluted in the fermenter. (See the examples that follow.) When the OG of the boil is less than 1.050, then the correction factor is equal to 1.0. (The factor can never be less than 1.0.) The correction factor is calculated as follows:

$$C_{gravity} = 1 + [(G_{boil} - 1.050)/0.2],$$

where G_{boil} equals the specific gravity of the wort in the boil kettle. For example, for a beer with a boil gravity of 1.090, $C_{gravity} = 1.2$.

If you do all this in metric units, it becomes a bit easier, since the conversion factor becomes 1,000. Here is an example:

$$IBU = \frac{W_{grams} \times U\% \times A\% \times 1,000}{V_{liters} \times C_{gravity}} \qquad (IBU\ \#2)$$

Table A provides some basic utilization values that any brewer can use as a starting point for estimating bitterness. They are based on professional data as well as general homebrewing experience. If you notice that your results consistently differ, then you should customize the utilization values for your own brewing conditions.

TABLE A

Basic Utilization Values

Boil Time (Minutes)	Whole Hop Utilization	Pellet Hop Utilization
Dry hop	0%	0%
0 to 9	5%	6%
10 to 19	12%	15%
20 to 29	15%	19%
30 to 44	19%	24%
45 to 59	22%	27%
60 to 74	24%	30%
75 or longer	27%	34%

Any recipe that includes more than one hop addition will require you to perform this calculation for each addition. This will become apparent from the examples that follow.

Examples

Let's work through an example of brewing pale ale, using these basic utilization values:

- OG of 1.048
- 1 ounce of 12.5% alpha-acid whole Chinook hops for 60 minutes
- 0.5 ounce of 4.4% alpha-acid whole Cascade hops for 15 minutes

The full volume will be boiled, and the target finished volume is 6 gallons.

Calculate the IBUs generated by each hop addition separately. First, calculate for the Chinooks, for which the variables would have the following values:

$$W_{oz} = 1 \qquad A\% = 0.125 \qquad U\% = 0.24$$
$$V_{gal} = 6 \qquad C_{gravity} = 1$$

Thus $\text{IBU} = \dfrac{1 \times 0.24 \times 0.125 \times 7{,}489}{6 \times 1} = 37.4$

For the Cascades addition, the variables are as follows:

$$W_{oz} = 0.5 \qquad A\% = 0.044 \qquad U\% = 0.12$$
$$V_{gal} = 6 \qquad C_{gravity} = 1$$

$$\text{IBU} = \dfrac{0.5 \times 0.12 \times 0.044 \times 7{,}489}{6 \times 1} = 3.3$$

Total IBUs for this recipe are 37.4 (from Chinook) + 3.3 (from Cascade) = 40.7.

Here's another example, this time using a bitter that is boiled at three gallons for dilution to five gallons in the fermenter. The target gravity is 1.040, so the gravity in the boil pot will be 1.066. Assume one hop addition, 1.5 ounces of 6.5% alpha-acid Willamette hops, 45 minutes before the end of the boil.

First, do the gravity correction:

$$C_{gravity} = 1 + [(1.066 - 1.050)/0.2] = 1.08$$

Now the other variables look like this:

$W_{oz} = 1.5$ $A\% = 0.065$

$U\% = 0.269$ $V_{gal} = 5$

The resulting equation is as follows:

$$IBU = \frac{1.5 \times 0.269 \times 0.065 \times 7{,}489}{5 \times 1.08} = 36.4$$

Using this basic equation, you can estimate IBUs quite accurately, provided the utilization values used are accurate for your brewery. Because the utilization values capture many characteristics of your brewing equipment and process, they can vary considerably from brewer to brewer.

Determining the Weight of Hops Required

You can turn this equation around to determine the weight of a specific hop required to give you a specific IBU level as follows.

In ounces and gallons:[1]

$$W_{oz} = \frac{V_{gal} \times C_{gravity} \times IBU}{U\% \times A\% \times 7,489}$$ (IBU #3)

In grams and liters:[2]

$$W_{grams} = \frac{V_{liters} \times C_{gravity} \times IBU}{U\% \times A\% \times 1,000}$$ (IBU #4)

List of North American Brown Ales and Their Brewers

This appendix, drawn from the *Beer Brand Index*, lists almost 350 brown ales made by brewers in the United States and Canada, in alphabetical order by brewery.

ALE	BREWERY
'Possum Trot Brown Ale	75th Street Brewery
Alaskan Arctic Ale	Alaskan Brewing and Bottling Co.
Naked Aspen Brown Ale	Alpine Brewing Co./Naked Aspen Beer Co.
Amber Waves Brown	Amber Waves Brewery and Pub
Dark Raspberry Ale	American River Brewing Co.
Nut Brown Ale	Amsterdam Brewing Co.
Harvest Brown Ale	Anacortes Brewhouse

Appendix B

ALE	BREWERY
Andrew's Brown Ale	Andrew's Brewing Co.
Shake Down Nut Brown	Angelic Brewing Co.
Barnum Island Brown	Atlantic Brewing Co.
Bar Harbor Real Ale	Atlantic Brewing Co./
	Lompoc Cafe Brewpub
Ancient Brown Ale	Atlantis Brewing Co.
Ellie's Brown Ale	Avery Brewing Co.
Thunder Hole Ale	Bar Harbor Brewing
Barrington Brown Ale	Barrington Brewery and Restaurant
Brown Bear Ale	Bear Brewing Co.
Barn Dog Brown Ale	Beier Brewing Co.
Battenkill Brown Ale	Bennington Brewers Ltd.
Nut Brown Ale	Big Horn Brewing Co. of Colorado/
	CB Potts
Metro Nut Brown	Big River Grille and Brewing Works
J Ross Brown Ale	Big River Grille and Brewing Works
Moose Drool	Big Sky Brewing Co.
Denali Ale	Bird Creek Brewery Inc.
Uptown Brown Ale	Bitter End Brewery
Oh Be Joyful Brown Ale	Black River Brew House
Nut Brown Ale	Blackstone Restaurant and Brewery
Prairie Dog Brown	Blind Tiger Brewery and Restaurant
Audrey's Brown	Blue Cat Brew Pub
Big Barley Brown	Blue Pine Brewpub Co.

ALE	BREWERY
Afton Ale	Blue Ridge Brewing Co.
Anniversary Ale	Bluegrass Brewing Co.
Brown Ale	Boardwalk Bistro
Market Street Nut Brown Ale	Bohannon Brewing Co./Market Street Brewery and Public House
Borealis Nut Brown Ale	Borealis Brewery
Beantown Nut Brown Ale	Boston Beer Works
Nuts Nut Brown Ale	Box Office Brewery
Brown Ale	Boyne River Brewing Co.
Brandywine Brown	Brandywine Brewing Co.
Griffon Brown Ale	Brasserie McAuslan
Uller Fest	Breckenridge Brewery and Pub
Ball Park Brown Ale	Breckenridge Brewery Denver
Dirty Water Boston Brown Ale	Brew Moon Enterprises
Bow Valley Brown	Brewsters Brewing Co. and Restaurant (No. 2)
Bow Valley Brown	Brewsters Brewing Co. and Restaurant/ Cornerstone Inn (No. 3)
Qu'Appelle Ale	Brewsters Brewing Co. and Restaurant/ Cornerstone Inn (No. 3)
Red Brick Ale	Bricktown Brewery
BridgePort Nut Brown Ale	BridgePort Brewing Co.
Brown Ale	Broad Ripple Brewing Co.
Brooklyn Brown	Brooklyn Brewery

Appendix B

ALE	BREWERY
Emerald Irish Ale	Burlingame Station Brewing Co./ Golden State Brewing Co.
Gary's Fat Tire	Cafe on the Square and Brewpub
Nameless Nut Brown	Callahan's Pub and Brewery
Northwest Nut Brown Ale	Capitol City Brewing Co.
Holiday Ale	Carmel Brewing Co.
Carnegie Hill Urban Ale	Carnegie Hill Brewing Co.
Carolina Nut Brown Ale	Carolina Brewing Co.
Colorado Trail Nut Brown Ale	Carver Brewing Co.
Home Run Ale	Champion Brewing Co.
Sweet Ginger Brown Ale	Chicago Brew Pub
TW Fisher's Nut Brown	Coeur d'Alene Brewing Co./ TW Fisher's Brewpub
Marmot Nut Brown Ale	Columbine Mill Brewery Inc.
Columbus Nut Brown Ale	Columbus Brewing Co.
Nut Brown Ale	Columbus Brewing Co.
Nut Brown	Commonwealth Brewing Co.
Dunraven Ale	CooperSmith's Pub and Brewing
Brown Ale	Copper Canyon Brewing/Ale House
Big Dog Brown	Copper Tank Brewing Co./ Austin Microbrewers LLC
Nutz	Coyote Springs Brewing Co. and Cafe
Vinolok Harvest Brown	Crested Butte Brewing Co./ Idle Spur Restaurant
English Bill's Half & Half Ale	Crown City Brewery

ALE	BREWERY
Buffalo Brown	Dave's Brewpub
Bond Street Brown Ale	Deschutes Brewery
Bond Street Brown Ale	Deschutes Brewery (No. 2)
Brown Ale	Dock Street Brewing Co. Brewery and Restaurant
Brown Ale	Duclaw Brewing Co.
Barrel-Roll Brown	Duster's Micro-brewery
Chestnut Brown Ale	Eddie McStiff's Brewpub
Midtown Brown	El Dorado Brewing Co.
Buchan Nut Brown	Ellicotville Brewing Co./S & W Co. LLC
Nut Brown Ale	Emerald Isle Brew Works Ltd.
Drake's Crude Ale	Erie Brewing Co./Hoppers Brewpub
Brown Eyed Ale	Eske's Brew Pub/Sangre de Cristo Brewing Co.
Bantam Brown	Eugene City Brewing Co./ West Brothers Bar-B-Q
Faultline Brown Ale	Faultline Brewing Co. Inc.
Brown Eyed Girl	Firehouse Brewing Co.
Brown Cow Ale	Firehouse Brewing Co.
Catfish Brown Ale	Fish Brewing Co./Fishbowl Pub
Nordenskjold Nut Brown	Flagstaff Brewing Co.
Flat Branch Brown Ale	Flat Branch Brewing Co.
Rin Tin Tan	Flying Dog Brewpub
Bullmastiff	Flying Dog Brewpub
Blue Ridge Hop Fest	Frederick Brewing Co.

ALE	BREWERY
John Brown Ale	Free State Brewing Co.
Gale Force Ale	Front Street Ale House/ San Juan Brewing Co.
Whale Ale	Front Street Ale House/ San Juan Brewing Co.
Full Sail Brown Ale	Full Sail Brewpub and Tasting Room
Beer Down Nut Brown	Gentle Ben's Brewing Co.
Nut Brown	Gold Coast Brewing Co.
Lion's Pride	Golden Lion Pub and Brewing Co.
Golden Prairie Nut Brown Ale	Golden Prairie Brewing Co.
Brown Ale	Golden Valley Brewery & Pub
Hex Nut Brown Ale	Goose Island Brewing Co.
Sugarbush Brown Ale	Grand Rapids Brewing Co.
Cleveland Brown Ale	Great Lakes Brewing Co.
Greenshields Nut Brown	Greenshields Brewery and Pub
Lion's Pride Brown Ale	Gritty McDuff's
Nuptial Ale	Gritty McDuff's
McDuff's Best Brown Ale	Gritty McDuff's (No. 2)
Horace Wells Brown Ale	Hartford Brewery Ltd.
Flag Me Down Brown	Harvest Moon Brewery/The Ales Co./ Sullivan Brewing
Dog's Breath Brown Ale	Heavenly Daze Brewery & Grill
Nut Brown	Heritage Brewing Co.
Nut Brown	Highland Pub and Brewery/McMenamin's
Thunderhead	Highland Pub and Brewery/McMenamin's

ALE	BREWERY
Balcone's Fault Red Granite	Hill Country Brewing and Bottling Co.
Bruin	Himmelberger Brewing Co.
Buffalo Brown Ale	Hoffbrau Steaks Brewery
Old Porch Dog Ale	Hoppers Brooker Creek/
	Grille and Taproom
A1 Ale	Hops Grill and Bar in Orange Park
Nut Brown Ale	Horseshoe Bay Brewing Co. Ltd.
Oyster Ale	Horseshoe Bay Brewing Co. Ltd.
Two Parrots Premium Ale	Horseshoe Bay Brewing Co. Ltd.
Downtown Brown	Hubcap Brewery and Kitchen
Beaver Tail Brown Ale	Hubcap Brewery and Kitchen
Slow Down Brown	Il Vicino Wood Oven Pizza
Tenderfoot Brown Ale	Il Vicino Wood Oven Pizza (No. 2)
Ipswich Dark Ale	Ipswich Brewing Co.
Buffalo Brown Ale	Jackson Hole Pub and Brewery/
	Snake River Brewing Co.
Nut Brown Ale	Jaipur Restaurant and Brewpub
Burly Brown Ale	James Page Brewing Co.
Chihuahua Pale Ale	Jaxson's Restaurant and Brewing Co.
Georgia Nut Brown Ale	John Harvard's Brewhouse (No. 2)/
	The Brew House LLC
Nut Brown Ale	John Harvard's The Brew House/
	The Brew House LLC
Johnson's Authentic Brown Ale	Johnson Beer Co.
Nut Brown Ale	Joseph Huber Brewing Co.

ALE	BREWERY
Brown Ale	Judge Baldwin's Brewing Co./
	BF Coleman Brewing Corp.
Bell's Best Brown Ale	Kalamazoo Brewing Co. Inc.
Downtown after Dark	Karl Strauss Breweries
Dry Hopped Brown Ale	Karl Strauss Breweries
Brown Ale	Katie Bloom's/Irish Pub and Brewery
Moose Brown Ale	Kennebunkport Brewing Co.
Crown Brown Ale	King Brewing Co.
Brown Ale	La Taverne du Sergeant
Brown Ale	Lafayette Brewing Co.
Main Beach Brown Ale	Laguna Beach Brewing Co.
Tahoe Nutty Winter	Lake Tahoe Brewing Co. Inc.
Good Medicine	Lang Creek Brewery
Ruby Brown Ale	Latchis Grille and Windham Brewery
Brune	Le Cheval Blanc
Legend Brown Ale	Legend Brewing Co.
Nutsy Fagan	Liberty Street Brewing Co.
Sigmund's Nut Brown	Library Restaurant and Brewing Co.
Drake's Ale	Lind Brewing Co.
Drake's Brown Ale	Lind Brewing Co.
Scottish Light	L'Inox
Nut Brown Ale	Los Gatos Brewing Co.
Downtown Brown Ale	Lost Coast Brewery & Cafe
Winterbraun Ale	Lost Coast Brewery & Cafe

ALE	BREWERY
Plantation	Louisiana Brewing Co./
	Brasserie de la Louisiane
Derby City Dark	Louisiana Jack's/Silo Brewpub
Barleyhopper Brown	MJ Barleyhoppers Brewery and Sports Pub
Nut Brown Ale	Mad Monk Brewing Co. Ltd.
Main Street Brown Ale	Main Street Brewing Co.
Downtown Brown	Market Street Pub
Downtown Brown Ale	Martha's Exchange
Double Diamond Dark	Martha's Exchange
Buckeye Boys Brown	Maumee Bay Brewing Co.
Brundage Brown	McCall Brewing Co./Cerveceria Inc.
Nut Brown	McMenamin's/Murray and Allen
Professor Brewhead's	McNeill's Brewery
Old-Fashioned Ale	
Slopbucket Brown	McNeill's Brewery
Joust a Brown Ale	Middle Ages Brewing Co. Ltd.
Middlesex Brown Ale	Middlesex Brewing Co. Inc.
Kodiak Brown	Midnight Sun Brewing Co.
Oktoberfest Ale	Mill Brewery, Bakery & Eatery
Knute Brown Ale	Mishawaka Brewing Co.
Long Trail Brown Ale	Mountain Brewers Inc.
Brown Dog Ale	Mountain Sun Pub and Brewery
Ruffian Nut Brown Ale	Mountain Valley Brewpub
Downtown Brown	Norman Brewing Co.

ALE	BREWERY
Old Brown Dog	Northampton Brewery/Brewster Court Bar & Grill
Nutfield "Bally Gally" Brown Ale	Nutfield Brewing Co.
Nut Brown Ale	Oak Creek Brewing Co.
Leroy Brown	Oaken Barrel Brewing Co.
Tut Brown Ale	Oasis Brewery and Restaurant
Tut Brown Ale	Oasis Brewery Annex
Brown Ale	Okanagan Spring Brewery
Brown	Old Baldy Brewing Co.
Broadway Brown	Old Broadway
Old Town Brown Ale	Old Colorado Brewing Co.
Four Barn Brown	Old Hampton Brewers Ltd.
Pilgrim Nut Brown Ale	Old Harbor Brewing Co. (The Pilgrim Brewery)
Old Peninsula	Olde Peninsula Brewpub Downtown Brown
Meriwether's Best Brown	Onalaska Brewing Co.
Nut Brown Ale	Oregon Ale and Beer Co.
Nut Brown	Oregon Trader Brewing Co.
Oregon Trail Brown Ale	Oregon Trail Brewery
Rio Grande Brown	O'Ryan's Tavern & Brewery/ Oregon Mountain Brewing Co.
Honey Nut Brown Ale	Overland Park Brewing Co.
Little Bear Brown	Overland Stage Stop Brewery

ALE	BREWERY
Brown Ale	Pacific Hop Exchange
Pancho Villa Brown Ale	Padre Island Brewing Co.
Park Slope Nut Brown Ale	Park Slope Brewing Co.
Brewers Monkey Brown Ale	Pepperwood Bistro
Pete's Wicked Ale	Pete's Brewing Co.
Downtown Brown Ale	Phantom Canyon Brewing Co.
Thomas Jefferson Brown Ale	Philadelphia Brewing Co./
	Samuel Adams Brewhouse
Frederick's Town Brown	Picaroons Brewing Co.
Pinehurst Long Iron Brown Ale	Pinehurst Village Brewery
101 Nut Brown	Pizza Port/Solana Beach Brewery
Barley's Nutty Brown	Pony Express Brewing Co.
Oktoberfest	Portland Brewing Co.
Old Brown Dog	Portsmouth Brewery
Walnut Brown Ale	Prescott Brewing Co.
Pyramid Best Brown Ale	Pyramid Ales
Narrow Gauge	Railway Brewing Co.
Brown Ale	Randy's Restaurant and Fun
	Hunter's Brewery
Clipper's Brown Ale	Rattlesnake Creek Brewery
Brown Nut Ale	Red Rock Brewing Co.
Winterhook	Redhook Ale Brewery (No. 2)
Tied House Dark	Redwood Coast Brewing Co.
Brown Ale	Richbrau Brewing Co.

ALE	BREWERY
Brown Porter	Ringneck Brewing Co./
	The Brew Kettle Inc.
Bravo Brown Ale	Rio Bravo Restaurant & Brewery
Brown Ale	River City Brewing Co.
Old Town Brown	River City Brewing Co.
D Brown Ale	River City Brewing Co.
#119 Ale (Brown Ale)	Riverside Brewing Co.
Molly's Titanic Brown Ale	Rock Bottom Brewery
Big Horn Nut Brown	Rock Bottom Brewery (No. 2)
Big Horn Brown Ale	Rock Bottom Brewery (No. 3)
Big Horn Nut Brown	Rock Bottom Brewery (No. 4)
Pelican Brown Ale	Rock Bottom Brewery (No. 5)
Buzzard Brown Ale	Rock Bottom Brewery at Cleveland (No. 8)
Indian Summer Nut Brown Ale	Roosters 25th St. Brewing Co.
RSB Northern England Style	Routh Street Brewery
Brown Ale	
Nut Brown Ale	Rubicon Brewing Co.
Grizzly Nut Brown	Sailor Hagar's Brewpub
Saint Arnold Brown Ale	Saint Arnold's Brewing Co.
Schlafly Nut Brown Ale	Saint Louis Brewery/Schlafly Brands
East Kent Brown Ale	Salt Lake Brewing Co./Fuggles
Holiday Nut Brown Ale	Salt Lake Brewing Co./Fuggles
East Kent Brown Ale	Salt Lake Brewing Co./Squatters Pub
Holiday Nut Brown Ale	Salt Lake Brewing Co./Squatters Pub

ALE	BREWERY
Old Town Nut Brown	San Diego Brewing Co.
Barbary Coast Ale	San Francisco Brewing Co.
Nut Brown Ale	San Marcos Brewery and Grill
Dave's Delicious Dark	San Marcos Brewery and Grill
Old Town Nut Brown	Santa Barbara Brewing Co.
Santa Fe Nut Brown Ale	Santa Fe Brewing Co.
Prairie Dark Ale	Saskatoon Brewing Co./
	Cheers Roadhouse Inn
Sea Dog Old Gollywobbler	Sea Dog Brewing Co. (No. 2)
Brown Ale	
Nut Brown Ale	Seabright Brewery Inc.
New Dublin Brown Ale	Seven Barrel Brewery Shop
Brady's Brown Ale	Shannon Kelly's Brewpub
Brown Ale	Shed Restaurant and Brewery
Channel Island Storm	Shields Brewing Co.
Milford Brown Ale	Ship Inn Inc.
Moose Brown Ale	Shipyard Brewing Co.
Downtown Brown Ale	Sioux Falls Brewing
Steelie-Brown Ale	Skagit River Brewing Co.
Nut Brown Ale	slo Brewing Co. Inc.
Slopeside Brown Ale	Slopeside Brewing Co.
Nut Brown Ale	Smoky Mountain Brewing Co.
Old Brown Dog	Smuttynose Brewing Co.
Bad Bear Brown Ale	Sonoma Brewing Co.

ALE	BREWERY
Pointe Nut Brown Ale	South Pointe Seafood House and Brewing Co.
South Shore Nut Brown Ale	South Shore Brewery
Mount Tolmie Dark	Spinnakers Brewpub Inc.
Jane's Brown Ale	Steamboat Brewery and Tavern
Summit Winter Ale	Summit Brewing Co.
Red Stone Ale	Sunday River Brewing Co.
Baron's Brown Ale	Sunday River Brewing Co.
Appleton Brown Ale	Swans
Brick House Brown Ale	Syracuse Suds Factory
TD's Nut Brown Ale	Table Rock Brewing Inc.
TD's Nut Brown Ale	Table Rock Brewpub and Grill
Groomal Growl	Taylor Brewing Co.
Beggar's Brown	Taylor Brewing Co.
New Moon Brown	Taylor Brewing Co.
Baggin's Brown	Taylor Brewing Co.
Beehive Brown	Telluride Beer Co.
Brown	Tied House Cafe and Brewery (No. 3)
Maple Nut Brown Ale	Tommyknocker Brewery & Pub
Otter Tail Brown Ale	Trader & Trapper
Brown Ale	Trinity Beer Works Inc.
Triumph Brown Ale	Triumph Brewing Co./Disch Brewing Co.
Sid Brown Ale	Troy Brewing Co.
Pecan Nut Brown	Tulsa Brewing Co.

North American Brown Ales

ALE	BREWERY
Bowser's Brown	Twenty Tank Brewery
Mild Brown	Twin Falls Brewing Co./Muggers Brewpub
Pecan Nut Brown Ale	TwoRows Restaurant and Brewery
Nutbrown	Uinta Brewing Co.
Downtown Brown	Umpqua Brewing Co.
Hampton Brown Ale	Village Brewery
Wachusett Country Nut Brown Ale	Wachusett Brewing Co.
Old Elk Brown Ale	Walnut Brewery
Ben's Brown Ale	Waterloo Brewing Co.
Chuckanut Brown Ale	Whatcom Brewery
Black Tusk Ale	Whistler Brewing Co.
Montana Nut Brown	Whitefish Brewing Co.
Whitetail Brown Ale	Whitetail Brewing Inc.
Beaver Nut Brown	Wild Duck Brewery and Restaurant
Snow Goose Winter Ale	Wild Goose Brewery
Wild River Nut Brown Ale	Wild River Brewing and Pizza Co.
Nut Brown Ale	Wild River Brewing and Pizza Co. (No. 2)
Grampa Clem's Brown Ale	Winthrop Brewing Co.
Cane Country Brown Ale	Woodstock Brewing Co.
Frank's Nut Brown Ale	Yaletown Brewing Co.
Ybor Brown Ale	Ybor City Brewing Co.
Sara's Brown Ale	Yegua Creek Brewing Co.
Honcho Grande Ale	Yellow Rose Brewing Co.
Nut Brown	Yorkville Brewery & Tavern

Unit Conversion Chart

Index	lb. to kg	oz. to g	fl. oz. to ml
0.25	0.11	7	7
0.50	0.23	14	15
0.75	0.34	21	22
1.00	0.45	28	30
1.25	0.57	35	37
1.50	0.68	43	44
1.75	0.79	50	52
2.00	0.91	57	59
2.25	1.02	64	67
2.50	1.13	71	74
2.75	1.25	78	81
3.00	1.36	85	89
3.25	1.47	92	96
3.50	1.59	99	103
3.75	1.70	106	111
4.00	1.81	113	118
4.25	1.93	120	126
4.50	2.04	128	133
4.75	2.15	135	140
5.00	2.27	142	148
5.25	2.38	149	155
5.50	2.49	156	163
5.75	2.61	163	170
6.00	2.72	170	177
6.25	2.84	177	185
6.50	2.95	184	192
6.75	3.06	191	200
7.00	3.18	198	207
7.25	3.29	206	214
7.50	3.40	213	222
7.75	3.52	220	229
8.00	3.63	227	237
8.25	3.74	234	244
8.50	3.86	241	251
8.75	3.97	248	259
9.00	4.08	255	266
9.25	4.20	262	274
9.50	4.31	269	281
9.75	4.42	276	288
10.00	4.54	283	296
10.25	4.65	291	303
10.50	4.76	298	310
10.75	4.88	305	318
11.00	4.99	312	325
11.25	5.10	319	333
11.50	5.22	326	340
11.75	5.33	333	347
12.00	5.44	340	355

By Philip W. Fleming and Joachim Schüring. Reprinted with permission from *Zymurgy*®.

gal. to l US	gal. to l UK	qt. to l US	qt. to l UK	pt. to l US	pt. to l UK	tsp. to ml	tbsp. to ml	cup to ml
0.95	1.14	0.24	0.28	0.12	0.14	1.2	3.7	59
1.89	2.27	0.47	0.57	0.24	0.28	2.5	7.4	118
2.84	3.41	0.71	0.85	0.35	0.43	3.7	11.1	177
3.79	4.55	0.95	1.14	0.47	0.57	4.9	14.8	237
4.73	5.68	1.18	1.42	0.59	0.71	6.2	18.5	296
5.68	6.82	1.42	1.70	0.71	0.85	7.4	22.2	355
6.62	7.96	1.66	1.99	0.83	0.99	8.6	25.9	414
7.57	9.09	1.89	2.27	0.95	1.14	9.9	29.6	473
8.52	10.23	2.13	2.56	1.06	1.28	11.1	33.3	532
9.46	11.36	2.37	2.84	1.18	1.42	12.3	37.0	591
10.41	12.50	2.60	3.13	1.30	1.56	13.6	40.2	651
11.36	13.64	2.84	3.41	1.42	1.70	14.8	44.4	710
12.30	14.77	3.08	3.69	1.54	1.85	16.0	48.1	769
13.25	15.91	3.31	3.98	1.66	1.99	17.3	51.8	828
14.19	17.05	3.55	4.26	1.77	2.13	18.5	55.4	887
15.14	18.18	3.79	4.55	1.89	2.27	19.7	59.1	946
16.09	19.32	4.02	4.83	2.01	2.42	20.9	62.8	1,005
17.03	20.46	4.26	5.11	2.13	2.56	22.2	66.5	1,065
17.98	21.59	4.50	5.40	2.25	2.70	23.4	70.2	1,124
18.93	22.73	4.73	5.68	2.37	2.84	24.6	73.9	1,183
19.87	23.87	4.97	5.97	2.48	2.98	25.9	77.6	1,242
20.82	25.00	5.20	6.25	2.60	3.13	27.1	81.3	1,301
21.77	26.14	5.44	6.53	2.72	3.27	28.3	85.0	1,360
22.71	27.28	5.68	6.82	2.84	3.41	29.6	88.7	1,419
23.66	28.41	5.91	7.10	2.96	3.55	30.8	92.4	1,479
24.60	29.55	6.15	7.39	3.08	3.69	32.0	96.1	1,538
25.55	30.69	6.39	7.67	3.19	3.84	33.3	99.8	1,597
26.50	31.82	6.62	7.96	3.31	3.98	34.5	103.5	1,656
27.44	32.96	6.86	8.24	3.43	4.12	35.7	107.2	1,715
28.39	34.09	7.10	8.52	3.55	4.26	37.0	110.9	1,774
29.34	35.23	7.33	8.81	3.67	4.40	38.2	114.6	1,834
30.28	36.37	7.57	9.09	3.79	4.55	39.4	118.3	1,893
31.23	37.50	7.81	9.38	3.90	4.69	40.7	122.0	1,952
32.18	38.64	8.04	9.66	4.02	4.83	41.9	125.7	2,011
33.12	39.78	8.28	9.94	4.14	4.97	43.1	129.4	2,070
34.07	40.91	8.52	10.23	4.26	5.11	44.4	133.1	2,129
35.01	42.05	8.75	10.51	4.38	5.26	45.6	136.8	2,188
36.96	43.19	9.99	10.80	4.50	5.40	46.8	140.5	2,248
37.91	44.32	9.23	11.08	4.61	5.54	48.1	144.2	2,307
37.85	45.46	9.46	11.36	4.73	5.68	49.3	147.9	2,366
38.80	46.60	9.70	11.65	4.85	5.82	50.5	151.6	2,425
39.75	47.73	9.94	11.93	4.97	5.97	51.8	155.3	2,484
40.69	48.87	10.17	12.22	5.09	6.11	53.0	159.0	2,543
41.64	50.01	10.41	12.50	5.20	6.25	54.2	162.6	2,602
42.58	51.14	10.65	12.79	5.32	6.39	55.4	166.3	2,662
43.53	52.28	10.88	13.07	5.44	6.53	56.7	170.0	2,721
44.48	53.41	11.12	13.35	5.56	6.68	57.9	173.7	2,780
45.42	54.55	11.36	13.64	5.68	6.82	59.1	177.4	2,839

Chapter References

Chapter 1. The History of Brown Ale

1. John P. Arnold, *The Origin of Beer and Brewing* (Chicago: Alumni Association of the Wahl-Henius Institute of Fermentology, 1911), 362.
2. H. Stopes, *Malt and Malting* (London: F. W. Lyon, 1855), 6.
3. H. S. Corran, *A History of Brewing* (London: David & Charles, 1975), 28.
4. Ibid., 30.
5. Anonymous, *One Hundred Years of Brewing* (New York: Arno Press, 1974), 24.
6. Judith M. Bennett, *Ale, Beer, and Brewsters in England: Women's Work in a Changing World, 1300–1600* (New York: Oxford University Press, 1996), 17.
7. Corran, *A History of Brewing*, 29.
8. Bennett, *Ale, Beer, and Brewsters in England*, 25.
9. Corran, *A History of Brewing*, 29.
10. Bennett, *Ale, Beer, and Brewsters in England*, 79.
11. Ibid., 19.
12. Corran, *A History of Brewing*, 50–51, 32.
13. Ibid., 32.
14. Ibid., 96.
15. Ibid.
16. Gervase Markham, *The English Housewife* (1615; reprint, McGill Queens University Press, 1986), 285.
17. William Harrison and Georges Edelen, *The Description of England: The Classic Contemporary Account of Tudor Social Life* (Dover Publications, 1995).

18. Stopes, *Malt and Malting*, 30–31.
19. Cindy Renfrow quoted this excerpt from Markham's *The English Housewife* through personal communication of July 2, 1998.
19. Ibid.
20. Corran, *A History of Brewing*, 80.
21. Bennett, *Ale, Beer, and Brewsters in England*, 79.
22. Corran, *A History of Brewing*, 50–51.
24. Bennett, *Ale, Beer, and Brewsters in England*, 85.
25. Ibid.
26. Ibid.
27. Corran, *A History of Brewing*, 51.
28. Bennett, *Ale, Beer, and Brewsters in England*, 77.
29. *The Compact Edition of the Oxford English Dictionary* (New York: Oxford University Press, 1971), 324.
30. Ibid., 626.
31. Cindy Renfrow, *A Sip through Time: A Collection of Old Brewing Recipes* (self-published, 1995), 3–4.
32. Ibid., 4.
33. Ibid., 6.
34. Ibid., 7–15.
35. J. Harrison, et al., *An Introduction to Old British Beers and How to Make Them*, 2d ed. (The Durden Park Beer Circle, 1991), 21, 24.
36. Corran, *A History of Brewing*, 111.
37. Peter Mathias, *The Brewing Industry in England 1700–1830* (Cambridge: Cambridge University Press, 1959), 14–15.
38. Corran, *A History of Brewing*, 108.
39. Corran, *A History of Brewing*, 106.
40. Stopes, *Malt and Malting*, 30–31.
41. Mathias, *The Brewing Industry in England 1700–1830*, 184.

42. Ibid.

43. Harrison, *An Introduction to Old British Beers and How to Make Them*, 32.

44. John Tuck, *The Private Brewer's Guide to the Art of Brewing Ale and Porter* (1822; reprint, Woodbridge, Conn.: Zymoscribe, 1995), 167.

45. Harrison, *An Introduction to Old British Beers and How to Make Them*, 38.

46. George Stewart Amsinck, *Practical Brewings: A Series of Fifty Brewings* (London: self-published, 1868), 158.

47. Renfrow, *A Sip through Time*, 20.

48. John Hull Brown, *Early American Beverages* (New York: Bonanza Books, 1966), 70.

49. David Sutula, "Mild Ale—Back from the Brink of Extinction?," *Brewing Techniques* 5, no. 6 (December 1997): 26.

50. Robert Wahl and Max Henius, *American Handy Book of the Brewing, Malting and Auxiliary Trades*, 3rd ed. (Chicago: Wahl-Henius Institute, 1908), 1,251.

51. B. Meredith Brown, *The Brewer's Art*, 2d ed. (London: Whitbread & Co. Ltd. by the Naldrett Press Ltd., 1949), 51; P. H. T. Evans, "The Brewing Industry in Britain," *Tagezeitung Brauerei* 68 (1971): 326–327; C. L. Duddington, *Plain Man's Guide to Beer* (London: Pelham Books, 1975); Pete Slosberg, "The Road to an American Brown Ale," *Brewing Techniques* 3, no. 3 (1995): 34.

52. Personal communication with R. H. Drury on July 9, 1998.

53. Wahl and Henius, *American Handy Book of the Brewing, Malting and Auxiliary Trades*, 1,253.

54. H. Lloyd Hind, *Brewing Science and Practice*, vol. 2 (London: Chapman and Hall, 1948), 545.

References

Chapter 2. Brown Ale Profile: It's Brown, It's an Ale— Are We Going Too Fast for You?

1. Geoff Cooper personally communicated the anonymously written *Beer Style Descriptions,* the updated version circulated by the National Guild of Wine and Beer Judges.
2. Ibid.
3. Ibid.
4. American Homebrewers Association, "Official 1992 AHA National Homebrew Competition Rules and Regulations," *Zymurgy* 14, no. 5 (Winter 1991), 5–7.
5. American Homebrewers Association, "1997 National Homebrew Competition Rules and Regulations," *Zymurgy* 19, no. 5 (Winter 1996), 1–10.

Chapter 3. Brewing Brown Ales

1. Ray Daniels, *Designing Great Beers: The Ultimate Guide to Brewing,* Classic Beer Styles Series (Boulder, Colo.: Brewers Publications, 1996), 227.
2. Ibid., 226.
3. L. W. Aurand, A. E. Woods, and M. R. Wells, *Food Composition and Analysis* (New York: Van Nostrand Reinhold Company), 207.
4. Ibid.
5. C. Bailey, "Make Mine with Molasses," *Zymurgy* 14, no. 4 (Special Issue 1994): 102–103.
6. J. Frane, "How Sweet It Is—Brewing with Sugar," *Zymurgy* 17, no. 1 (Spring 1994): 38–41.
7. Aurand, Woods, and Wells, *Food Composition and Analysis,* 161–164.

Chapter 4. Brown Ale Procedures

1. Hind, *Brewing Science and Practice*, 722–723.
2. J. S. Hough, D. E. Briggs, R. Stevens, and T. W. Young, *Malting and Brewing Science*, vol. 2 (London: Chapman & Hall, 1982), 673.
3. Hind, *Brewing Science and Practice*, 817.
4. Ibid.
5. Ray Daniels, *The Perfect Pint: Producing Real Ale in America*, 2d ed. (Chicago: Craft Beer Institute, 1998), 16.

Chapter 6. Enjoying Brown Ale

1. Stephen Beaumont, *Stephen Beaumont's Brewpub Cookbook: 100 Great Recipes from 30 Famous North American Brewpubs* (Boulder, Colo.: Siris Books, 1998).
2. J. Frane, "How Sweet It Is—Brewing with Sugar," 38–41.
3. L. W. Aurand, A. E. Woods, M. R. Wells, *Food Composition and Analysis*.

Appendix 1. Calculating International Bitterness Units

1. J. Rager, "Calculating Hop Bitterness in Beer," *Zymurgy* 13, no. 4 (Special Edition 1990): 53.
2. Ibid.

Glossary

acrospire. The germinal plant growth of the barley kernel.

ad-humulone. The third (or sometimes second) most prevalent of the three alpha acids, which, when isomerized during boiling of the wort, provides most of the bittering characteristic that comes from hops.

adjunct. Any unmalted grain or other fermentable ingredient added to the mash.

adjuncts. Sources of fermentable extract other than malted barley. Principally corn, rice, wheat, unmalted barley, and glucose (dextrose).

aerate. To force atmospheric air or oxygen into solution. Introducing air to the wort at various stages of the brewing process.

aeration. The action of introducing air to the wort at various stages of the brewing process.

aerobic. In the presence of or requiring oxygen.

airlock. *See* fermentation lock.

airspace. *See* ullage.

albumin. Intermediate soluble protein subject to coagulation upon heating. Hydrolyzed to peptides and amino acids by proteolytic enzymes.

alcohol by volume (ABV). The percentage of volume of alcohol per volume of beer. To calculate the approximate volumetric alcohol content, subtract the final gravity from the original gravity and divide the result by 75. For example: 1.050 − 1.012 = 0.038/0.0075 = 5% ABV.

alcohol by weight (ABW). The percentage weight of alcohol per volume of beer. For example, 3.2% alcohol by weight = 3.2 grams of alcohol per 100 centiliters of beer. Alcohol by weight can be converted to alcohol by volume by multiplying by 0.795.

aldehyde. An organic compound that is a precursor to ethanol in a normal beer fermentation via the EMP pathway. In the presence of excess air, this reaction can be reversed, with alcohol being oxidized to very complex, unpleasant-tasting aldehydes, typically papery, cardboardy, sherry notes. These compounds are characterized as oxidized alcohols, with a terminal CHO group.

ale. 1. Historically, an unhopped malt beverage. 2. Now, a generic term for hopped beers produced by top fermentation, as opposed to lagers, which are produced by bottom fermentation.

aleurone layer. The enzyme- and pentosan-bearing layer enveloping, and inseparable from, the malt endosperm.

all-extract beer. A beer made with only malt extract as opposed to one made from barley or a combination of malt extract and barley.

all-grain beer. A beer made with only malted barley as opposed to one made from malt extract or from malt extract and malted barley.

alpha-acid unit (AAU). The number of AAUs in a hop addition is equal to the weight of the addition in ounces times the alpha-acid percentage. Thus 1 ounce of 5% alpha-acid hops contain 5 AAUs. AAU is the same as homebrewers bittering units.

alpha acid (a-acid). The principle source of bitterness from hops when isomerized by boiling. These separate but related alpha acids come from the soft alpha resin of the hop. (When boiled, alpha acids are converted to iso-alpha-acids.)

ambient temperature. The surrounding temperature.

amino acids. The building blocks of proteins. Essential components of wort, required for adequate yeast growth. They are the smallest product of protein cleavage. Simple nitrogenous matter.

amylodextrin. From the diastatic reduction of starch. Amylodextrins or a-limit dextrins. The most complex dextrin from the hydrolysis of starch with diastase. Mahogany (red-brown) color reaction with iodine.

amylolysis. The enzymatic reduction of starch to soluble fractions.

amylopectin. Branched starch chain. Shell- and paste-forming starch. Unable to be entirely saccharified by amylolytic enzymes, so a-limit dextrins, or amylodextrins, remain.

amylose. Straight chain of native starch. Glucose dehydrate (a-D-glucose) molecules joined by a-(1-4) links. Gives deep blue-black color with iodine.

anaerobic. Conditions under which there is not enough oxygen for respiratory metabolic function. Anaerobic microorganisms are those that can function without the presence of free molecular oxygen.

apparent attenuation. A simple measure of the extent of fermentation that a wort has undergone in the process of becoming beer. Using gravity units (GU), degrees Balling (°B), or degrees Plato (°P) to express gravity, apparent attenuation is equal to the original gravity (OG) minus the terminal gravity divided by the OG. The result is expressed as a percentage and equals 65 to 80% for most beers.

apparent extract. The terminal gravity of a beer.

aqueous. Of water.

attemper. To regulate or modify the temperature.

attenuate. To reduce the extract/density by yeast metabolism.

attenuation. The reduction in the wort's specific gravity caused by the transformation of sugars into ethanol and carbon dioxide gas.

autolysis. Yeast death due to shock or nutrient-depleted solutions.

bacteriostatic. Bacteria inhibiting.

Balling. A saccharometer invented by Carl Joseph Napoleon Balling in 1843. A standard for the measurement of the density of solutions. It is calibrated for 63.5 °F (17.5 °C), and graduated in grams per 100, giving a direct reading of the percentage of extract by weight per 100 grams solution. For example, 10 °Balling = 10 grams of cane sugar per 100 grams of solution.

beerstone. Brownish gray mineral-like deposits left on fermentation equipment. Composed of calcium oxalate and organic residues.

blow-by (blow-off). A single-stage homebrewing fermentation method in which a plastic tube is fitted into the mouth of a carboy, with the other end submerged in a pail of sterile water. Unwanted residues and carbon dioxide are expelled through the tube, while air is prevented from coming into contact with the fermenting beer, thus avoiding contamination.

body. A qualitative indicator of the fullness or mouthfeel of a beer. Related to the proportion of unfermentable long-chain sugars or dextrins present in the beer.

Brettanomyces. A genus of yeasts that have a role in the production of some beers, such as modern *lambics* and Berliner *weisse* and historical porters.

brewer's gravity (SG). *See* gravity.

BU:GU ratio. The ratio of bitterness units (BU) to gravity units (GU) for a specific beer or group of beers. International bitterness units (IBU) are used for bitterness, and gravity units (GU) are used for the gravity component. GU = original gravity − 1 × 1,000. For most beers and beer styles, the resulting ratio has a value between 0.3 and 1.

buffer. A substance capable of resisting changes in the pH of a solution.

carbonates. Alkaline salts whose anions are derived from carbonic acid.

carbonation. The process of introducing carbon dioxide gas into a liquid by (1) injecting the finished beer with carbon dioxide; (2) adding young fermenting beer to finished beer for a renewed fermentation (kraeusening); (3) priming (adding sugar or wort) to fermented wort prior to bottling, thereby creating a secondary fermentation in the bottle; or (4) finishing fermentation under pressure.

carboy. A large glass, plastic, or earthenware bottle.

caryophylline. A secondary component of hop oil found in varying proportions in different varieties of hops.

cellulose. A polymer of sugar molecules that plays a structural rather than storage role. The sugars that make up cellulose cannot be liberated by the enzymes found in most plant systems.

chill haze. Haziness caused by protein and tannin during the secondary fermentation.

chill-proof. Cold conditioning to precipitate chill haze.

clarigen finings. Carrageen-based finings.

closed fermentation. Fermentation under closed, anaerobic conditions to minimize risk of contamination and oxidation.

co-humulone. The second (or sometimes third) most prevalent of the three alpha acids, which, when isomerized during the boiling of the wort, provide most of the bittering characteristic that comes from hops.

coliform. Waterborne bacteria, often associated with pollution.

colloid. A gelatinous substance in solution.

decoction. Boiling, the part of the mash that is boiled.

density. The measurement of the weight of a solution, as compared to the weight of an equal volume of pure water.

dextrin. Soluble polysaccharide fraction from hydrolysis of starch by heat, acid, or enzyme.

diacetyl. *See* diketone.

diacetyl rest. A warm—55 to 70 °F (13 to 21 °C)—rest that occurs during fermentation. During the diacetyl rest, yeast metabolize diacetyl and other byproducts of fermentation.

diastase. Starch-reducing enzymes. Usually alpha- and beta-amylase, but also limit dextrinase and a-glucosidase (maltase).

diastatic malt extract. A type of malt extract containing the diastatic enzymes naturally found in malt and needed for conversion of starch into sugar. This type of extract is sometimes used in recipes that contain grain adjuncts such as corn or rice.

diketone. A class of aromatic, volatile compounds perceivable in minute concentrations, from yeast or *Pediococcus* bacteria metabolism—most significantly, the butter and butterscotch aroma of diacetyl, a vicinal diketone (VDK). The other significant compound relevant to brewing is 2,3-pentanedione.

dimethyl sulfide (DMS). An important sulfur-carrying compound originating in malt. Adds a crisp, "lager-like" character at low levels and corn or cabbage flavors at high levels.

disaccharides. Sugar group. Two monosaccharide molecules joined by the removal of a water molecule.

dry hopping. The addition of hops to the primary fermenter, the secondary fermenter, or to casked beer to add aroma and hop character to the finished beer without adding significant bitterness.

dry malt. Malt extract in powdered form.

European brewery convention (EBC). *See* SRM.

enzymes. Protein-based organic catalysts that affect changes in the compositions of the substances they act on.

erythrodextrin. Tasteless intermediate dextrin. Large a-limit dextrins. Faint red reaction with iodine.

essential oil. The aromatic volatile compounds from the hop.

ester. A class of organic compounds created from the reaction of an alcohol and an organic acid. These tend to have fruity aromas and are detectable at low concentrations.

esters. "Ethereal salts" such as ethyl acetate. Aromatic compounds from fermentation composed of an acid and an alcohol, such as the "banana" ester. Formed by yeast enzymes from an alcohol and an acid. Associated with ale and high-temperature fermentations, esters also arise to some extent with pure lager yeast cultures, though more so with low wort oxygenation, high initial fermentation temperatures, and high-gravity wort. Top-fermenting yeast strains are prized for their ability to produce particular mixes of esters.

extract. The amount of dissolved materials in the wort after mashing and lautering malted barley and/or malt adjuncts such as corn and rice.

extraction. Drawing out the soluble essence of the malt or hops.

farnescene. A secondary component of hop oil found in varying proportions in different varieties of hops.

fermentation lock. A one-way valve that allows carbon dioxide gas to escape from the fermenter while excluding contaminants.

final specific gravity. The specific gravity of a beer when fermentation is complete.

fining. (n.) A clarifying agent. (v.) The process of adding clarifying agents to beer during secondary fermentation to precipitate suspended matter. Examples of clarifying agents are isinglass, gelatin, bentonite, silica gel, or polyvinyl pyrrolidone.

flocculation. The tendency of yeast to clump together at the end of fermentation. The greater the tendency for the yeast to flocculate, the faster it will drop out of the solution, thereby creating clearer or brighter beer.

germination. Sprouting of the barley kernel to initiate enzyme development and conversion of the malt.

glucophilic. An organism that thrives on glucose.

gravity (SG). Specific gravity as expressed by brewers. Specific gravity 1.046 is expressed as 1046. Density of a solution as compared to water. Expressed in grams per milliliter (1 milliliter water weighs 1 gram, hence sp. gr. 1.000 = SG 1000; sp. gr. 1.046 = SG 1046).

gravity units (GU). A form of expressing specific gravity in formulas as a whole number. It is equal to the significant digits to the right of the decimal point (1.055 SG becomes 55 GU and 1.108 SG becomes 108 GU).

green malt. Malt that has been steeped and germinated and is ready for kilning.

gruit. A mixture of spices and herbs used to bitter and flavor ales before the acceptance of hops as a bittering and flavoring agent.

hemocytometer. A device used for counting blood cells (or brewer's yeast) under a microscope.

hexose. Sugar molecules of six carbon atoms. Includes glucose, fructose, lactose, mannose, and galactose.

homebrewers bittering units (HBU). A formula adopted by the American Homebrewers Association to measure bitterness of beer. Example: 1.5 ounces of hops at 10% alpha acid for 5 gallons: 1.5 × 10 = 15 HBU per 5 gallons. Same as alpha-acid unit (AAU).

homofermentive. Organisms that metabolize only one specific carbon source.

hop pellets. Hop cones compressed into tablets. Hop pellets are 20 to 30% more bitter by weight than the same hop variety in loose form. Hop pellets are less subject to alpha-acid losses than are whole hops.

humulene. A primary component of the essential oil of the hop cone. Although rarely found in beer in this native form, it is processed into a number of flavor-active compounds that are significant in beer. The quantity of humulene found in a hop varies by variety, year, and growing region.

humulone. The most prevalent of the three alpha acids, which, when isomerized during boiling of the wort, provides most of the bittering characteristic that comes from hops.

hydrolysis. Decomposition of matter into soluble fractions by either acids or enzymes in water.

hydrometer. A glass instrument used to measure the specific gravity of liquids as compared to water, consisting of a graduated stem resting on a weighted float.

hydroxide. A compound, usually alkaline, containing the OH (hydroxyl) group.

inoculate. The introduction of a microbe into surroundings capable of supporting its growth.

international bitterness unit (IBU). This is a standard unit that measures the concentration of iso-alpha-acids in milligrams per liter (parts per million). Most procedures will also measure a small amount of uncharacterized soft resins, so IBUs are generally 5 to 15% higher than iso-alpha-acid concentrations.

isinglass. A gelatinous substance made from the swim bladder of certain fish and added to beer as a fining agent.

isomer (iso). Organic compounds of identical composition and molecular weight but having a different molecular structure.

kilning. The final stage in the malting of barley that prepares it for use by the brewer. Kilning reduces the moisture contained in the grain to approximately 4% and also roasts the malt to some extent. The degree of roasting affects the flavor and color of the malt as well as of the beer it produces.

kraeusen. (n.) The rocky head of foam that appears on the surface of the wort during fermentation. Also used to describe the period of fermentation characterized by a rich foam head. (v.) To add fermenting wort to fermented beer to induce carbonation through a secondary fermentation.

Lactobacillus. Species of bacteria that ferments wort sugars to produce lactic acid. Although considered undesirable in most breweries and beer styles, it plays a significant role in the production of some beers, such as Berliner *weisse* and *lambics*.

lactophilic. An organism that metabolizes lactate more readily than glucose.

lager. (n.) A generic term for any bottom-fermented beer. Lager brewing is now the predominant brewing method worldwide except in Britain, where top-fermented ales dominate. (v.) To store beer at near-freezing temperatures in order to precipitate yeast cells and proteins and improve taste.

lauter. The process of separating the clear liquid from the spent grain and husks.

lauter tun. A vessel in which the mash settles and the grains are removed from the sweet wort through a straining process. It has a false slotted bottom and spigot.

lipids. Fatlike substances, especially triacylglycerols and fatty acids. Negatively affect a beer's ability to form a foam head. Cause soapy flavors and, when oxidized, contribute stale flavors.

liquefaction. The process by which alpha-amylase enzymes degrade soluble starch into dextrin.

malt. Barley that has been steeped in water, germinated, and then dried in kilns. This process converts insoluble starches to soluble substances and sugars.

malt extract. A thick syrup or dry powder prepared from malt.

maltose. A disaccharide composed of two glucose molecules. The primary sugar obtained by diastatic hydrolysis of starch. One-third the sweetness of sucrose.

mashing. Mixing ground malt with water to extract the fermentables, degrade haze-forming proteins, and convert grain starches to fermentable sugars and nonfermentable carbohydrates.

melanoidins. Color-producing compounds produced through a long series of chemical reactions that begin with the combination of a sugar and an amino acid.

methylene blue. A stain used to test the viability (ability to reproduce) of a yeast cell.

modification. 1. The physical and chemical changes that occur in barley during malting where complex molecules are broken down to simpler, soluble molecules. 2. The degree to which malt has undergone these changes, as determined by the growth of the acrospire. The greater the degree of modification, the more readily available starch is and the lower the protein level is.

mole. A unit of measure for chemical compounds. The amount of a substance that has a weight in grams numerically equal to the molecular weight of the substance. Also, gram-molecular weight.

myrcene. A primary component of the essential oil of the hop cone. Although rarely found in beer in this native form, it is processed into a number of flavor-active compounds that are significant in beer. The quantity of myrcene found in a hop varies by variety, year, and growing region.

original gravity. The specific gravity of wort previous to fermentation. A measure of the total amount of dissolved solids in wort.

oxidation. 1. The combining of oxygen with other molecules, often causing off-flavors, as with oxidized alcohols, to form aldehydes. 2. A reaction in which the atoms in an element lose electrons and its valence is correspondingly increased (oxidation-reduction reaction).

parti-gyle. An arcane system of brewing in which the first runnings of wort are taken to make a high-gravity beer and the grain is then remashed to create another brew. This can be done yet again to make a third brew, all from the same grains. There is usually no sparging involved when using the parti-gyle system. With the advent of more sophisticated equipment that allowed lautering and sparging, the parti-gyle system of brewing lost favor around the end of the nineteenth century.

pectin. Vegetable/fruit substance. A chain of galacturonic acid that becomes gelatinous in the presence of sugars and acids.

pentosan. Pentose-based complex carbohydrates, especially gums.

pentose. Sugar molecules of five carbon atoms. Monosaccharides.

peptonizing. The action of proteolytic enzymes upon protein, successively yielding albumin/proteoses, peptides, and amino acids.

pH. A measure of acidity or alkalinity of a solution, usually on a scale of 1 to 14, where 7 is neutral.

phenols. Aromatic hydroxyl precursors of tannins/polyphenols. "Phenolic" in beer describes medicinal flavors from tannins, bacterial growth, cleaning compounds, or plastics.

phosphate. A salt or ester of phosphoric acid.

pitching. Inoculating sterile wort with a vigorous yeast culture.

Plato, degrees. Commercial brewers' standard for the measurement of the density of solutions, expressed as the equivalent weight of cane sugar in solution (calibrated on grams of sucrose per 100 grams of solution). Like degrees Balling, but Plato's computations are more exact.

Plato saccharometer. A saccharometer that expresses specific gravity as extract weight in a 100-gram solution at 68 °F (20 °C). A revised, more accurate version of Balling, developed by Dr. Plato.

polymer. A compound molecule formed by the joining of many smaller identical units. For example, polyphenols from phenols and polypeptides from peptides.

polyphenol. Complexes of phenolic compounds involved in chill-haze formation and oxidative staling.

polysaccharides. Carbohydrate complexes, able to be reduced to monosaccharides by hydrolysis.

ppm. Parts per million. Equal to milligrams per liter (mg/l). The measurement of particles of matter in solution.

precipitation. Separation of suspended matter by sedimentation.

precursor. The starting materials or inputs for a chemical reaction.

primary fermentation. The first stage of fermentation, during which most fermentable sugars are converted to ethyl alcohol and carbon dioxide.

priming. The act of adding priming sugar to a still (or flat) beer so that it may develop carbonation.

priming solution. A solution of sugar in water added to aged beer at bottling to induce fermentation (bottle conditioning).

priming sugar. A small amount of corn, malt, or cane sugar added to bulk beer prior to racking or at bottling to induce a new fermentation and create carbonation.

protein. Generally amorphous and colloidal complex amino acid containing about 16% nitrogen with carbon, hydrogen, oxygen, and possibly sulfur, phosphorous, and iron. True protein has a molecular weight of 17,000 to 150,000. In beer, protein will have been largely decomposed to a molecular weight of 5,000 to 12,000 (albumin or proteoses), 400 to 1,500 (peptides), or amino acids. Protein as a haze fraction ranges from molecular weight 10,000 to 100,000 (average 30,000) and as the stabilizing component of foam, from 12,000 to 20,000.

proteolysis. The reduction of protein by proteolytic enzymes to fractions.

racking. The process of transferring beer from one container to another, especially into the final package (bottles, kegs, and so on).

reagent. A substance involved in a reaction that identifies the strength of the substance being measured.

real ale. A style of beer found primarily in England, where it has been championed by the consumer rights group called the Campaign for Real Ale (CAMRA). Generally defined as a beer that has undergone a secondary fermentation in the container from which it is served and that is served without the application of carbon dioxide.

resin. Noncrystalline (amorphous) plant excretions.

rest. Mash rest. Holding the mash at a specific temperature to induce certain enzymatic changes.

ropy fermentation. Viscous gelatinous blobs, or "rope," from bacterial contamination.

rousing. Creating turbulence by agitation. Mixing.

runnings. The wort or sweet liquid that is collected during the lautering of the wet mash.

saccharification. The naturally occurring process in which malt starch is converted into fermentable sugars, primarily maltose. Also called mashing, since saccharification occurs during the mash rest.

saccharometer. An instrument that determines the sugar concentration of a solution by measuring the specific gravity.

secondary fermentation. 1. The second, slower stage of fermentation, which, depending on the type of beer, lasts from a few weeks to many months. 2. A fermentation occurring in bottles or casks and initiated by priming or by adding yeast.

sparge. The even distribution or spray of hot water over the saccharified mash to rinse free the extract from the grist.

sparging. Spraying the spent grains in the mash with hot water to retrieve the remaining malt sugar. This is done at the end of the mashing (saccharification) process.

specific gravity. A measure of a substance's density as compared to that of water, which is given the value of 1.000 at 39.2 °F (4 °C). Specific gravity has no accompanying units because it is expressed as a ratio. Specific gravity is the density of a solution in grams per milliliter.

standard reference method (SRM) and **European brewery convention (EBC).** Two different analytical methods of describing color developed by comparing color samples. Degrees SRM, approximately equivalent to degrees Lovibond, are used by the ASBC (American Society of Brewing Chemists), while degrees EBC are European units. The following equations show approximate conversions: $(EBC) = 2.65 \times (SRM) - 1.2$; $SRM = 0.377 \times (EBC) + 0.46$.

starch. A polymer of sugar molecules. The chief form of energy storage for most plants. It is from starch that the relevant sugars for brewing are derived.

starter. A batch of fermenting yeast added to the wort to initiate fermentation.

steeping. The initial processing step in malting, where the raw barley is soaked in water and periodically aerated to induce germination.

strike temperature. The initial (target) temperature of the water when the malted barley is added to it to create the mash.

substratum. The substance in or on which an organism grows.

tannin. Astringent polyphenolic compounds, capable of colliding with proteins and either precipitating or forming haze fractions. Oxidized polyphenols form color compounds relevant in beer. *See also* polyphenol.

terminal extract. The density of the fully fermented beer.

titration. Measurement of a substance in solution by the addition of a standard disclosing solution to initiate an indicative color change.

trisaccharide. A sugar composed of three monosaccharides joined by the removal of water molecules.

trub. Flocks of haze-forming particles resulting from the precipitation of proteins, hop oils, and tannins during the boiling and cooling stages of brewing.

turbidity. Sediment in suspension. Hazy, murky.

ullage. The empty space between a liquid and the top of its container. Also called airspace or headspace.

viscosity. The resistance of a fluid to flow.

volatile. Readily vaporized, especially esters, essential oils, and higher alcohols.

volume of beer. To calculate the approximate volumetric alcohol content, subtract the terminal gravity from the original gravity and divide the result by 75. For example: $1.050 - 1.012 = 0.038/0.75 = 0.05$ or 5% ABV.

water hardness. The degree of dissolved minerals in water. Usually expressed in parts per million (ppm) or grains per gallon (gpg).

wort. Mash extract (sweet wort). The hopped sugar solution before pitching, before it is fermented into beer.

Bibliography

Amsinck, George Stewart. *Practical Brewings: A Series of Fifty Brewings.* London: Self-Published, 1868.

The London and Country Brewer. 1750. Dublin, U.K.

One Hundred Years of Brewing. 1903. A Supplement to *The Western Brewer.* H. S. Rich & Co., Publishers.

"Beer Style Descriptions." Undated. National Guild of Wine and Beer Judges. Conveyed to the authors by Geoff Cooper.

Arnold, John P. *Origin and History of Beer and Brewing.* Alumni Association of the Wahl-Henius Institute of Fermentology. Chicago, 1911.

Beaumont, Stephen. *Stephen Beaumont's Brewpub Cookbook.* Boulder, Colo.: Siris Books, 1998.

Bennett, Judith M. *Ale, Beer, and Brewsters in England: Women's Work in a Changing World, 1300–1600.* Oxford University Press, 1996.

Briess Malting Co. *Briess Web Page.* Chilton, Wis., 1997.

Brown, B. Meredith. *The Brewer's Art.* Second edition. London: Whitbread & Co., Ltd., by the Naldrett Press, Ltd., 1949.

Brown, John Hull. *Early American Beverages.* New York: Bonanza Books, 1966.

Corran, H. S. *A History of Brewing.* London: David & Charles, 1975.

Crisp, William. Personal communication, 1998.

Daniels, Ray. *Designing Great Beers.* Boulder, Colo.: Brewers Publications, 1996.

Duddington, C. L. *Plain Man's Guide to Beer.* London: Pelham Books, 1975.

Bibliography

Evans, P. H. T. "The Brewing Industry in Britain." *Tageszeitung Brauerei* 68 (1971): 326–327.

Fix, George. *Principles of Brewing Science*. Boulder, Colo.: Brewers Publications, 1989.

Fix, George and Laurie Fix. *An Analysis of Brewing Techniques*. Boulder, Colo.: Brewers Publications, 1997.

Foster, Terry. *Pale Ale*. Boulder, Colo.: Brewers Publications, 1990.

——— . *Porter*. Boulder, Colo.: Brewers Publications, 1992.

Frane, J. "How Sweet It Is—Brewing with Sugar." *Zymurgy* 17, no. 1 (Spring 1994).

Harrison, J., et al. *An Introduction to Old British Beers and How to Make Them*. Second Edition. The Durden Park Beer Circle, 1991.

Harrison, John. "Dr. J. C. Harrison of the Durden Park Beer Circle Looks at Amber Ale, a Beer That Has Always Been Easy to Drink, but Hard to Define." *The Grist* (1996).

Haydon, Peter. *The English Pub: A History*. London: Robert Hale Ltd., 1994.

Hind, H. Lloyd. *Brewing Science and Practice, Volume Two: Brewing Processes*. Third Impression. London: Chapman & Hall Ltd., 1948.

Hough J. S., D. E. Briggs, R. Stevens, and T. W. Young. *Malting and Brewing Science, Volume 2: Hopped Wort and Beer*. London: Chapman and Hall, 1982.

Institute for Brewing Studies. *Beer Brand Index*. Boulder, Colo.: 1996.

Jackson, Michael. *Michael Jackson's Beer Companion*. Philadelphia: Running Press, 1993.

———. *Michael Jackson's World Guide to Beer*. Philadelphia: Running Press, 1987.

Korzonas, Al. *Homebrewing: Volume I*. Palos Hills, Ill.: Sheaf and Vine, 1997.

LaPensee, Clive. *The Historical Companion to House-Brewing.* Beverly, U.K., 1990.

Markham, Gervase. "The English Housewife." First published in 1615. The new edition, ed. by Michael R. Best, 1986.

Mathias, Peter. *The Brewing Industry in England 1700–1830.* Cambridge University Press, 1959.

Miller, Dave. *Brewing the World's Great Beers.* Pownal, Vt.: Storey Books, 1992.

———. *The Complete Handbook of Home Brewing.* Pownal, Vt.: Storey Books, 1989.

Mosher, Randy. *The Brewer's Companion,* revised ed. Seattle: Alephenalia Publications, 1995.

Noonan, Gregory. *New Brewing Lager Beer.* Boulder, Colo: Brewers Publications, 1996.

Oliver, Garrett. "A Brown Ale Comeback." *All About Beer* (July 1997).

Renfrow, Cindy. *A Sip through Time: A Collection of Old Brewing Recipes.* Sussex, N.J.: Self-Published, 1995.

Scottish and Newcastle Breweries. *Newcastle Brown Ale Web Page.* Newcastle Upon Tyne, 1996. Web address is http://www.broonale.co.uk.

Shaw, A. H. A posting to the historical brewing mailing list, 1995.

Slosberg, Pete. "The Road to an American Brown Ale." *Brewing in Styles* column, Martin Lodahl, Column Editor. *Brewing Techniques,* Vol. 3, No. 3 (1995): 46.

Slosberg, Pete. Personal communication, 1997.

Stopes, H. *Malt and Malting.* London: F. W. Lyon, 1885.

Sutula, David. "Mild Ale—Back from the Brink of Extinction?" Martin Lodahl, Column Editor. *Brewing Techniques.* Vol. 5, No. 6 (December 1997).

The Compact Edition of the Oxford English Dictionary. Oxford: Oxford University Press, 1971.

Tuck, John. *The Private Brewer's Guide to the Art of Brewing Ale and Porter*. London, 1822. Reprinted by ZymoScribe, Woodbridge, Conn., 1995.

Wahl, Robert and Max Henius. *American Handy Book of the Brewing, Malting, and Auxiliary Trades*. Third Edition. Chicago: Wahl-Henius Institute, 1908.

Walker, Dennis. "Age Clarity and Smoke in Medieval Beers." A posting on the historical brewing mailing list, 1997.

Wheeler, Graham and Roger Protz. *Brew Classic European Beers at Home*. Ann Arbor, Mich.: G. W. Kent, 1997.

Index

Please note that page references in italic indicate photographs.

Index

Index

Index

Index

About the Authors

Ray Daniels, award-winning author of *Designing Great Beers* and *101 Ideas for Homebrew Fun*, is an accomplished craftbrewer with both home and professional brewing experience. He is a top graduate of Siebel Institute's diploma course in brewing and is president and founder of the Craft Beer Institute. As a well-known authority on brewing, Ray travels throughout the world teaching

beer evaluation and brewing courses to professional and hobby brewers. Ray and his family currently live in Chicago.

Jim Parker, an award-winning homebrewer, has been involved in almost every facet of the brewing world, from

head brewer at a brewpub to being one of the original staff members of America's first regional brewspaper. Jim presently resides in Colorado's Front Range, where he is managing partner of the Wolf Tongue Brewery in the mountain town of Nederland.